BEES AND MANKIND

A 16th-century hive and bees.

BEES AND MANKIND

John B. Free

London
GEORGE ALLEN & UNWIN
Boston   Sydney

George Allen & Unwin (Publishers) Ltd,
40 Museum Street, London WC1A 1LU, UK

George Allen & Unwin (Publishers) Ltd,
Park Lane, Hemel Hempstead, Herts HP2 4TE, UK

Allen & Unwin Inc.,
9 Winchester Terrace, Winchester, Mass 01890, USA

George Allen & Unwin Australia Pty Ltd,
8 Napier Street, North Sydney, NSW 2060, Australia

First published in 1982

British Library Cataloguing in Publication Data

Free, John
    Bees and mankind.
1. Bees
I. Title
595.79′9   QZ568.A6
ISBN 0–04–638001–9

Library of Congress Cataloging in Publication Data

Free, John Brand.
    Bees and mankind.
1. Bees.   2. Bee culture – History.   I. Title.
QL568.A6F548   1982   595.79′9   82–11319
ISBN 0–04–638001–9 (pbk.)

Set in 11 on 13 point Times by Nene Phototypesetters Ltd, Northampton
and printed in Great Britain
by Alden Press, Oxford, London and Northampton

For Nicola with love

Preface

This book attempts to provide an account of the biology of bees, especially those with which man is associated, and to trace man's interest in them from prehistoric times to the present day.

It is written in the hope that the reader will become as fascinated by bees and beekeeping as I am, and will appreciate the extent of our indebtedness to the bee. There is a great need to conserve and replenish populations of wild bees, and to encourage the use of honey-bees not only for producing honey and wax, but for pollinating our crops and wild flowers, so enhancing the bounty and beauty of our world.

It gives me pleasure to thank those who have generously helped me. The Rev. R. Darchen and Dr W. P. Nye have kindly allowed me to reproduce their photographs.

I am indebted to R. Creighton (former President, British Beekeepers Association), W. E. J. Hooper (Beekeeping Instructor, County of Essex, England), S. C. Jay (Professor and Head of Department of Entomology, University of Manitoba, Canada) and E. C. Martin (former Professor of Entomology, Michigan State University, and co-ordinator of United States Department of Agriculture bee research programmes) for kindly reading and criticising the manuscript and for correcting mistakes and pointing out omissions; the faults remaining are entirely my responsibility.

I am grateful to Miles Jackson, Life Sciences Sponsor, George Allen & Unwin, for the enthusiasm and sustained interest which he has shown during the preparation of this book for publication.

Finally, my wife Nancy deserves my thanks for her help in preparing the manuscript and selecting the illustrations, and especially for her understanding and encouragement.

JOHN B. FREE
Harpenden, 1982

Acknowledgements

I would like to thank the following individuals and organisations who have given me permission to reproduce illustrations:

Figure 3.19 reprinted from Karl von Frisch: *Bees, their vision, chemical senses and language*, copyright 1950 by Cornell University; used by permission of the publisher, Cornell University Press, and by permission of Jonathan Cape Ltd. Figure 3.21 reprinted from Karl von Frisch: *Bees, their vision, chemical senses and language*, revised edition, copyright 1950, copyright © 1971, by Cornell University; used by permission of the publisher, Cornell University Press, and by permission of Jonathan Cape Ltd. Figure 4.1 reprinted from Camargo, J. M. F. de 1970. Ninhos e biologia de algumas espécies de Meliponideos (Hymenoptera: Apidae) da regiâo de Pôrto Velho, Territorio de Rondônia, Brasil. *Revista de Biologia Tropical* **16**, 207–39, by permission of the Editor of that journal and Harvard University Press. Figure 5.1 reprinted from Dams, Lya R. 1978. Bees and honey-hunting scenes in the Mesolithic rock-art of eastern Spain. *Bee World* **59**, 45–53, by permission of the Editor of that journal and Lya R. Dams. Figure 5.2 reprinted from Pager, H. 1977. *Stone Age myth and magic as documented in the rock paintings of South Africa*. Graz: Akademische Druck-u. Verlagsanstalt, by permission of the publisher and author. Figure 5.3 reprinted from Pager, H. 1973. Rock paintings in Southern Africa showing bees and honey hunting. *Bee World* **54**, 61–8, by permission of the Editor of that journal and Harald Pager. Figure 6.1 reprinted from Ransome, H. 1937. *The sacred bee in ancient times and folk-lore*. London: George Allen & Unwin, by permission of the Editor, *British Bee Journal*. Figure 6.2 reproduced from a specimen in the Heraklion Museum, Crete. Figure 6.3 reprinted from Forster, K. A. 1975. *Die Biene*. Küsnacht-Zurich, by permission of the publishers. Figure 7.2 reprinted from Forster, K. A. 1975. *Die Biene*. Küsnacht-Zurich, by permission of the publishers and the Bibliothèque Nationale, Paris. Figure 7.3 reproduced by permission of the Bodleian Library, Oxford (MS. Bodley 764, folio 89 Bees). Figure 7.4 reprinted from Forster, K. A. 1975. *Die Biene*. Küsnacht-Zurich, by permission of the publishers and Collection Forster. Figure 7.5 reprinted from Marchenay, P. 1979. *L'homme et l'abeille*. Paris: Berger-Levrault, by permission of the Bibliothèque Nationale, Paris. Figure 9.1 reprinted from Jenyns, F. G. 1886. *A book about bees*. London: Wells, Gardner, Darton & Co., by permission of the publishers.

I would also like to thank the following individuals and organisations for permission to reproduce poetical quotations:

Extracts from 'The beekeeper's daughter' taken from *Colossus* by Sylvia Plath, and extracts from 'The bee meeting' and 'Stings' taken from *Ariel* by Sylvia Plath; both books published by Faber & Faber, London, copyright © 1967 and 1965 Ted Hughes. Extracts from 'The long trail' and 'The bee boy's song' from *Rudyard Kipling's verse: definitive edition* by Rudyard Kipling, reprinted by permission of Doubleday & Co., Inc., The National Trust and Macmillan London Ltd. Extracts from *The prophet* by Kahlil Gibran and from 'Bee master' in *The land* by V. Sackville West, reprinted by permission of Heinemann Ltd. Extract from 'The Lake Isle of Innisfree' from *Collected poems* of William Butler Yeats (New York: Macmillan 1956), reprinted by permission of M. B. Yeats, Anne Yeats, Macmillan London Ltd and Macmillan Publishing Co., Inc. Extract from 'The lost heifer' by Austin Clarke, reprinted by permission of the Dolmen Press.

Front cover   An alert honeybee worker standing guard at the nest entrance

Contents

Introduction

Go to the bee, then poet, consider her ways and be wise.
Bernard Shaw, *Man and Superman*

Bees have always fascinated man, who has long drawn comparisons between his own social life and that of the bee. However, only a small proportion of bees live in highly developed social organisations and all the transitional stages in the evolution of social behaviour can be traced in the many different types of solitary, semi-social and social bees that abound today.

The development of social behaviour usually includes prolongation of the life of the mother so that she can care for her developing young; change from total neglect to attentive feeding of the young; overlap of generations; development of non-reproductive individuals; and development of co-operation between the members of the colony. Examples will include various types of solitary bee, bumblebee, stingless bee and honeybee.

The honeybee colony is one of the most striking achievements of evolution, and its members exhibit the most complex behaviour known among invertebrates. The activities of the bees, including the way in which they defend their colonies and the division of labour among them, will be described. Examples of the close-knit relationship between bees and flowers and the way in which bees efficiently exploit the local flora will be illustrated. Recent findings have helped us to understand how the cohesion of the colony is maintained, and how the individuals communicate with each other so that the colony functions as an efficient unit.

Bees originally provided man with his sole source of sweetening material, and honey has long been credited with 'magical' properties. Honey hunting, as practised in parts of Africa today, is similar to that which existed in prehistoric times. Although bees have been kept in hives in Egypt and China for at least 4000 years, in different regions of the world today every example of beekeeping from the most primitive to the most sophisticated is still to be found.

In association with the general increase in interest in natural history in recent years, the interest in beekeeping has also greatly increased in North America and Europe. Moreover, because many of our wild pollinators are now scarce, the honeybee is often relied upon to pollinate our agricultural and horticultural crops. The bee is, and always has been, of great value to man: this book examines in detail man's debt to the bee.

1

Part I

Bees: solitary and social

The wild bee reels from bough to bough
With his furry coat and his gauzy wing,
Now in a lily-cup and now
Setting the jacinth bell a-swing.
Oscar Wilde, 'Her Voice'

Man has relatively few friends in the insect world, but notable among these are the bees, many of which are valuable, if not essential, in pollinating agricultural and horticultural crops. Without the pollinating services of bees, the world would certainly be a duller place; flowers dependent on insect visits would disappear; many wild plants, bushes and trees would fail to produce edible seed and fruit, and birds and mammals would suffer as a consequence. Indeed, bees are a vital link in the food chain of many animals, including man. The more we can learn about our bees, the more chance we have of being able to conserve them.

The most familiar bees are the social ones: the bumblebees, the stingless bees and the honeybees, which provide man with honey and wax. However, few people realise that in some ways these social bees are very much in the minority and form only about five per cent of a total of well over 20 000 bee species.

1 *Solitary bees*

But when was ever honey made
with one bee in a hive?

Thomas Hood, 'The Last Man'

The female of the vast majority of bee species makes her own nest or nests without help from any of her kind. These 'solitary bees' are found throughout the world from the Arctic Circle to the tip of South America, wherever there are suitable nesting sites and flowering plants to produce nectar and pollen.

There is much variation in the type of site that solitary bees choose for a nest. Most nest in the ground, digging tunnels with lateral branches in which the young develop. Favourable sites for such species may contain as many as 1000 nests in close proximity, but the females do not co-operate at all in their activities.

Other common solitary bee species burrow almost exclusively in plant material, including dead branches and stems of living plants, but will also on occasion use almost any suitable cavity. Yet others nest in galls, cones or fruit, or construct their nests on the outside of plant stems or under stones.

Having discovered or excavated her nest, each female sets about provisioning it. She visits flowers to collect loads of pollen, and different species of bee often have favourite flowers. Numerous hairs on her body facilitate the collection of pollen which she carries back to her nest on special pollen-carrying hairs on her rear legs or beneath her abdomen. Many of the hairs are branched. On return to her nest she deposits the pollen on the floor of the cell which she has prepared, and on it she lays an egg. As soon as this is accomplished, she seals off the cell and repeats the process. Thus each egg and its bed of pollen are enclosed in a separate cell. A variety of materials may be used to line the walls of the cells and to form the end walls separating one cell from another; they include chewed plant material, pieces of leaves or petals, fine plant fibres or soil mixed with saliva, the type selected depending again on the species.

When the egg hatches, the larva feeds on the pollen, which has to last throughout its entire developmental period. Hence this type of feeding is known as 'mass provisioning'. After they have finished feeding, the larvae enter a resting phase; the larvae of some species overwinter in this condition, while others overwinter as pupae or adults, but still within their cocoons. The adult bees do not emerge from the nest which 5 their mother made until spring or summer, when they mate and the whole process is repeated. Ordinarily, the mother bee dies before her young have matured into adults, and once she has laid eggs she has no more contact with her progeny. She is indeed a 'solitary' bee.

Because there is such a proliferation of solitary species it is impossible to select a 'typical' example. However, it will be interesting and instructive to consider the behaviour and life histories of a few types in more detail.

A *solitary bee:* Osmia rufa

> In burrows narrow as a finger, solitary bees keep house.
> Sylvia Plath,* 'The Beekeeper's Daughter'

Bees of the genus *Osmia* (family Megachilidae) occur in many parts of the world, probably largely because they have adapted to nesting in a variety of habitats, including the soil and man-made walls, as well as plant material. Some species of *Osmia* even have the unusual habit of nesting in empty snail-shells.

One species, *Osmia rufa*, which derives its specific name from the red hair covering its body, is particularly widespread and has been studied more than most.

In the spring, the individual bees which were reared the year before emerge from hibernation. Typically, the males emerge before the females, sometimes up to 3 weeks earlier, and while waiting for their prospective mates spend much of their time feeding on the nectar and pollen of flowers and in becoming sexually mature. They also establish a kind of territorial mating behaviour which we will meet again with the bumblebees.

Osmia rufa males spend much of their time resting in selected sites, such as crevices in a tree or building, or flying along distinct 'routes' from one such site to another. Often these sites are in the vicinity of the nests from which the females are still to emerge, or less often they are near flowers. Sometimes the route followed is from one resting site to another, followed by a direct return; sometimes the route embraces a number of such sites, the direction of flight being reversed after the final resting site has been reached; and sometimes the route may follow a circuit so that no resting place is visited more than once. Any females that are encountered are immediately chased, and when they alight they are pounced on and mated with. Whereas the males mate several times, the females mate once only; this leads to competition for females and

*Sylvia Plath was herself the daughter of O. E. Plath who wrote *Bumblebees and their ways*.

Figure 1.1 Solitary bee, *Osmia rufa*, foraging on oil seed rape.

fighting frequently occurs between males in the vicinity of the nests, the most dominant and aggressive occupying the favoured individual resting places. However, the lives of the males are short; soon after mating they die, and they take no part in nest building.

In contrast, after mating the real work of the female begins, and she soon searches for a suitable site in which to build a nest. *Osmia rufa* is catholic in its choice of nest-site and will commonly use sandy banks, and old decaying wood, and if necessary many man-made sites such as nail holes, defects in the mortar of old walls, and locks and tubing of various sorts.

Once a suitable nest site is located the female orientates carefully to it, while undertaking a series of gradually extending zig-zags and circles in front of the entrance, so that she will be able to locate it without difficulty on future occasions. She then proceeds to remove any debris from the nest interior before beginning to build the cells in which her young are to be reared. When possible these are arranged in a linear series and separated by partitions built of mud.

She collects the mud from damp soil at the edges of pools or puddles, by scraping it together with her mandibles and moulding it into a pellet against the underside of her abdomen, which she bends forward between her legs. In only about 40 seconds the pellet has grown sufficiently to be carried in her mandibles and forelegs back to the nest, where it is worked into the partition while still moist. About eight such pellets are needed to build each partition.

After building the cell wall the bee sets about provisioning the interior, and collecting food then occupies most of her time. For each

Solitary bees cell she needs to make about 20 foraging trips; the pollen is carried back to the nest in a brush of long hairs on the underside of her abdomen, and the nectar in the extended sac of her oesophagus known as the 'crop' or 'honey-stomach'.

On return to her nest the bee first regurgitates nectar on the pollen which it has collected previously, and kneads it into a stiff paste with her mandibles; she then turns around and uses both her rear legs to scrape the pollen off her abdomen. When the nest is narrow the bee cannot turn around to do this but reverses to the nest entrance, turns around and backs in again.

When the food mass is finally big enough and the bee has kneaded into its surface the last load of pollen, she turns around and lays an egg on it. Soon afterwards the bee leaves the nest to collect more mud to build the next partition. Under favourable conditions, a female *Osmia rufa* may complete one cell a day, and during her entire life about twenty or more.

Once a cell is completed the egg is effectively sealed in its cell with a food supply that has to suffice for its entire development. About a week after the egg has been laid the larva hatches, and in about another week the lower part of its body has become distended and the colour of the pollen it has consumed is clearly visible through its body wall.

About 30 days after hatching the larva starts to spin its cocoon and after another 2 weeks or so starts to change into a pupa; the dry faecal pellets of the larva become scattered over the wall of the cell. It is another 7 weeks or so before the adult bee finally emerges. This usually occurs in the autumn and the adult bee remains quiescent in its cocoon until the following spring.

Figure 1.2 Solitary bee, *Osmia rufa*, larvae in cells feeding on beds of pollen.

Figure 1.3 Solitary bee, *Osmia rufa*, adult ready to emerge from cell.

By supplying or withholding the sperm she carries, a bee can lay either fertilised eggs that produce females or unfertilised eggs that produce males. Female *Osmia rufa* are larger than the males, and need to eat more food and have more space for their development; the proportion of males to females depends on the diameters of the cells, and only male bees are produced in those as small as 5 mm in diameter.

The linear arrangement of the cells in a typical *Osmia rufa* nest necessitates that the bees in those near the entrance, which are the last to be constructed, are the first to emerge. However, they are not always the first to become active, especially as they are, of course, younger than those further back.

When a bee becomes active in the spring it bites through the cell partition towards the nest entrance, a process which takes a few hours. If it then finds itself in a cell with a still dormant bee, it bites through the cocoon and nips the abdomen of the occupant to goad it into activity! Should, for some reason, the recipient have died, the emerging bee will, if necessary, chew through its body and into the next cell. In nests that contain both males and females, the males are nearly always situated in cells near the nest entrance, so they always leave the nest first, followed by the slightly older and larger females, the oldest female of all being the last to leave.

Trap nests

My banks they are furnished with bees,
Whose murmur invites me to sleep.
William Shenstone, 'A Pastoral Ballad'

Solitary bees The nests of solitary bees are not always easy to find; one reason for mentioning *Osmia rufa* at some length is that it can readily be induced to use artificial nest-sites and thus be studied at leisure. Various types of artificial nest-site have been used. More than 50 years ago, the famous French naturalist J. H. Fabre found that *Osmia* species occupied glass tubes and reeds that he provided, and since that time others have used clay 'bricks', blocks of wood and expanded polystyrene into which holes have been bored, ventilation bricks, hollow elder and bramble stems, bamboo canes and drinking straws. To achieve most success these nests are suspended 2–3 m above the ground from branches of trees, fence posts or outbuildings where solitary bees are known to be present.

Sometimes the trap nests are occupied by bees that have a strong tendency to nest gregariously, and, in such circumstances, the population can expand rapidly. When a bee species that is a useful pollinator of commercial crops behaves in this manner it can be of great economic importance for mankind.

An important pollinator: Megachile rotundata

Like Oberon's meadows her garden is
Drowsy from dawn to dark with bees.

Walter de la Mare, 'A Widow's Weeds'

One such species is *Megachile rotundata*. In common with other leaf-cutting bees of the genus *Megachile*, the mandibles of this species are equipped with special shearing edges. These enable the bees quickly to

Figure 1.4 Solitary bee, *Megachile rotundata* foraging on alfalfa (photo by W. P. Nye).

cut out circular or oval sections of leaf which they carry, curled beneath their abdomens, back to their nests and use to build their nest cells. The oval leaf sections are skilfully interwoven to form the side walls of the cell, between ten and twenty pieces being needed for each cell, and the circular leaf sections are used to form the end walls.

An important pollinator

The leaf cutter, *Megachile rotundata*, was accidentally introduced to the eastern coast of North America from eastern Europe and western Asia in about 1930. Although it does not excavate its own burrows, it readily occupies and multiplies in a variety of nest-sites. From the eastern coast it followed in the wake of the pioneers and spread westwards, reaching the far side of North America in the 1950s.

Under natural conditions the adult bees emerge from hibernation in late May when the alfalfa (lucerne) crops on the western coastal areas are in flower, and the males find females that are basking in the sun and mate with them. Each female will mate once only, but the male can mate many times. When the female has found a suitable nesting site, often near the nest in which she was reared, she makes a series of tubes of leaf cuttings, mostly of alfalfa, lightly glued together with a salivary secretion.

She provisions each cell with a mixture of honey and pollen, also collected from alfalfa. On return from foraging she enters her cell head first and regurgitates the nectar load; she then backs out of the cell, turns round at the entrance, and backs into the cell to deposit her pollen. When the cell is about one-half to two-thirds filled she lays an egg in it, and seals it with a cap of three to ten circular leaf cuttings. She then

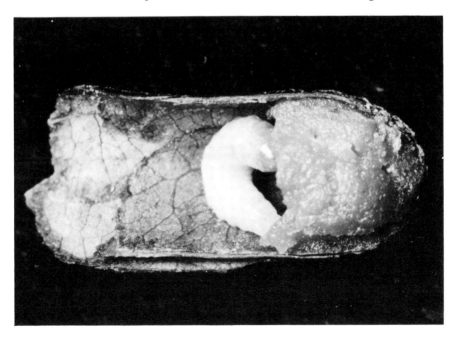

Figure 1.5 Solitary bee, *Megachile rotundata* larva feeding on store of pollen (photo by W. P. Nye).

starts to line and provision another cell until a series is built up to the entrance of the nest cavity. She finally plugs the end of the tunnel with many circular leaf cuttings, sometimes over a hundred of them.

Because in the alfalfa seed-growing areas of western North America *Megachile rotundata* collects leaf sections from alfalfa to line its nest cells, and also because it collects alfalfa nectar and pollen, it seemed to have the characteristics necessary to become a major pollinator of this important crop. Consequently, attempts were made to induce it to occupy man-made nests. These efforts were soon rewarded.

During the last two decades the seed yield of alfalfa crops provided with ample leaf-cutter pollinators has greatly increased, and *Megachile rotundata* has now become distributed to other parts of the world including Scandinavia, Chile, France and New Zealand.

Attempts are being made to discover more species of bee that can be exploited in this way, with the realisation that a bee may be more prolific and more useful to man as a pollinator when it is transferred to areas where it does not at present occur. It is hoped that these searches will yield favourable results before long.

Evolution of social life

> The bee enclosed and through the amber shown,
> Seems buried in the juice which was his own.
>
> Martial, *Epigrams*

Although bees like *Megachile rotundata* appear to be gregarious in nature, that is they nest in close proximity, they cannot be regarded as truly social. Although difficult to define precisely, social insects usually occur as a family or colony consisting of one or two parents and their off-spring sharing a common shelter, and co-operating with each other to at least some extent.

Unfortunately, the fossils of bees so far discovered are of little help in elucidating the evolutionary path followed by social bees, and it is only by studying the behaviour and organisation of present day bees that a probable series of steps can be traced from the most primitive solitary bees to the most advanced social bee, the honeybee.

Many so-called solitary bees exhibit social behaviour to some extent, and it is among some of the ground-nesting bees that we can easily see the beginnings of social life.

Each nest of bees belonging to the family Halictidae consists of a main vertical tunnel, from which branch lateral tunnels terminating in cells in which the brood is reared. The particular arrangement of the lateral tunnels and cells tends to be characteristic of the species concerned. The foundress bee spends much of her time and effort in excavating each nest; often this is done during the evening and night; she may need to moisten the soil with water before excavation is possible. She loosens each pellet of soil in turn and clasping it beneath her thorax carries it to the surface. The small mounds of soil that grow round each nest entrance are a testimony to its owner's industry. Once excavation is completed the female lines each cell with a wax-like varnish, provisioning it with a ball of nectar and pollen on which she lays an egg. The shape of the food mass, and its consistency, are characteristic of the species; the consistency can vary from almost dry to semi-liquid.

The tendency for many females to nest in close proximity is characteristic of several ground-nesting species, and the same location often contains hundreds or thousands of nests for several successive years. This gregarious habit is no doubt a response to a particularly favoured nest site, but it probably provides a real protective advantage favouring the survival of the species as a whole.

Although the females nest within a few centimetres of each other, each recognises and defends its own nest and there is no co-operation between them. However, it is possible that these nesting aggregations may indicate the first beginnings of social development. This stage could be followed in an evolutionary sequence by one in which more than one female uses the same nest entrance while still having her own lateral tunnels and cells, as do some species of *Halictus* today. This could then lead to a division of labour between females and eventually a differentiation into some females that lay eggs (the fertile females or 'queens') and some that remain sterile (the 'workers'). In this way the social structure could have arisen through a division of labour between adult females that were offspring of different parents.

The other possible way by which social life could have arisen is through co-operation between parent and offspring. This could only occur if the length of life of the female foundress increases sufficiently for her to remain alive to receive help from her first offspring to emerge. Once this prerequisite had been achieved it is possible to envisage a division of labour developing between the large female foundress and her smaller offspring, some of which remain sterile.

Increased longevity of the foundress and co-operation between bees also makes possible continuous care of the brood. Whereas primitive bees, as we have seen, practise mass provisioning in which an egg is laid on sufficient food to allow complete development to the adult stage, the more advanced insect societies feed the larvae progressively throughout their development according to their needs. No doubt intermediate stages of evolution occurred in which the workers exhibited an increased tendency to keep brood cells open and inspect and feed the occupants.

13

Solitary bees   Presumably increased care and attention diminishes brood mortality, but each stage must confer its own particular benefits, and stages towards the development of true social life are exemplified by various species of solitary and semi-social bee that exist today.

Whereas the first offspring, which are cared for solely by the foundress of a bee society or colony, may be relatively small sterile females, the later brood, reared with the help of the sterile females, is better nourished, and may develop into males and fertile females as large as the foundress, which eventually depart to produce colonies of their own.

This is approaching the level of social organisation shown by bumble-bees.

2 *Bumblebees*

Burly, dozing humble-bee,
Where thou art is clime for me,
Let them sail for Porto Rique,
Far-off heats through seas to seek;

I will follow thee alone,
Thou animated torrid-zone!

Wiser far than human seer,
Yellow-breeched philosopher!
Seeing only what is fair,
Sipping only what is sweet,

Thou dost mock at fate and care,
Leave the chaff and take the wheat.

Ralph Waldo Emerson, 'The Humble-Bee'

Bumblebees are among our largest and most colourful insects. They are at an evolutionary stage which in some ways is midway between that of the solitary bees and their more advanced relatives the honeybees. In contrast to most social insects they occur much more abundantly in temperate than in tropical climates, and are found in Europe, Asia, North Africa and in America as far north as the Arctic Circle and as far south as the tip of South America. They are not indigenous to Australasia, but a few species were successfully introduced to New Zealand at the end of the 19th century.

Emergence of queens from hibernation

Yet still the solitary humble-bee
Sings in the bean-flower.

Samuel Taylor Coleridge, 'The Lime Tree Bower My Prison'

In a temperate climate the story of a bumblebee colony begins in the spring with the emergence from hibernation of young females (known as 'queens') that were reared and mated the previous year. The appearance of the first queens coincides with the onset of warmer weather and the opening of the early spring flowers, and for the first few weeks the queens visit flowers to feed on the nectar and pollen. At night, and during cold weather, the queens take shelter beneath plant debris and become quite torpid until favourable conditions again occur. The

15

nourishment a queen obtains from flowers is essential, not only for her survival, but to develop her ovaries, which are small and threadlike when she emerges from hibernation. Indeed the presence of a succession of plentiful spring flowers is of paramount importance.

Selection of nest

> Said the bee to the mouse
> As he entered his house,
> Does it matter at all
> If your dwelling be small?
>
> Lorne Leigh, 'Amaranthe'

When the ovaries of a queen have developed sufficiently to contain eggs, she begins to search for a suitable site in which to found her colony, and it may take her several days or even weeks to discover one. It is while they are searching for nest sites that queen bumblebees are so conspicuous as they fly low along hedgerows, banks and rough ground, alighting every now and then to make a thorough investigation of a promising location. The site that a queen ultimately selects often contains the deserted nest of a mouse or other small mammal, which consists of pieces of grass, moss, leaves or other material accumulated by the former occupant.

An association between bumblebees and the nests of mice has long been recognised. Indeed, many years ago it was suggested that the wealth of Britain was founded on her cattle, and because these fed principally on red clover, which was pollinated by bumblebees, whose colonies occurred in the deserted nests of mice, whose rightful owners were killed by cats, which were kept by elderly spinsters, then it followed that the wealth of England was dependent on its spinster population!

The actual places in which a bumblebee queen looks for a nest-site depend very much upon her species. Some species seem to favour sites that are approached by underground tunnels, often several feet long, whilst others prefer sites with tunnels only a few inches in length. The queens of yet another species usually select nesting places on the surface of the ground, often under tussocks of grass, or under moss.

However, some species are fairly versatile in their habits and the nests of all species are occasionally found in a variety of habitats such as disused birds' nests, bundles of hay or straw, the thatch of cottages and barns, old upholstered furniture, garden rubbish, under the roots of decaying trees, the floors of outhouses and under concrete paths. Areas of uncultivated, infrequently disturbed land contain a much greater concentration of bumblebee nests than areas that are intensively cultivated. It is important, however, that the nest be in a dry, sheltered location.

> Often, if tales are true, they excavate snug nests
> And there below the ground keep house.
>
> H. F. Metcalf, 'The Bee Community'

When a queen has found a suitable nest, she pushes into its centre and forms an approximately circular chamber about 25 mm in diameter which she lines with fine nesting material. This chamber is connected to the outside by a tunnel through which she can just pass. On first leaving her new home, the queen makes a careful orientation flight during which she learns the position of her nest in relation to neighbouring objects and the features of the surrounding landscape.

For the next day or so the queen spends much time in the chamber where the warmth she produces begins to dry the nesting material. Occasionally she leaves the nest to forage for nectar which she carries home in her honey-stomach and deposits in the surrounding nest material. The nectar that the queen does not herself consume soon dries, and so helps to cement the nesting material together. Soon after completing her nest the queen starts to forage for pollen as well as nectar. On her return the pollen loads, which are carried in the special pollen baskets or 'corbiculae' on the queen's hind legs, are deposited on the floor of the nest cavity, where the queen uses her mandibles to mould them into a single lump. She needs to make several foraging trips before the lump is the right size, which varies from 6 to 10 mm in diameter according to the species concerned. All this time, the queen has been eating much pollen and, on this nutritious protein food, her ovaries have developed considerably, so that by the time she has collected sufficient pollen she is ready to lay her first eggs on the pollen lump. The method of deposition also differs with the species. Queens of some species lay their eggs so that they are vertically placed, each in its own small cavity within the pollen lump, while others deposit their eggs round the outside of the pollen lump.

As a result of consuming nectar the queen begins to produce wax, which issues as thin sheets from between the segments of her abdomen, especially on the dorsal surface. When egg laying is complete the queen uses the wax to build a canopy that completely encloses the pollen lump and eggs.

All subsequent egg batches are laid in wax cells that have already been prepared for them, and, in exceptional circumstances, the first egg batch is also laid on pollen that the queen has deposited in a shallow wax cup attached to the floor of the nest cavity. However, in all circumstances the eggs rest on a bed of pollen and are covered with a canopy of wax.

17

Figure 2.1 Bumblebee queen *Bombus hortorum* incubating her first batch of brood and facing the honeypot. She has established her colony while in captivity.

The number of eggs laid in the first batch varies with the different species of bumblebee and also, to some extent, from queen to queen within a species, but is generally between eight and fourteen. They are sausage-shaped, each about 3–4 mm long and 1 mm wide.

Once the eggs have been laid, the queen begins to build a wax pot just inside the entrance to the nest cavity; as soon as she has completed its base and the beginnings of its sides, she uses it to store nectar which she has collected in the field. It takes the queen a day or two to build her nectar pot, and when it is finished it may be up to 20 mm tall and 13 mm wide. The nectar that the queen stores in it provides a food reserve for her during the night and in bad weather when she cannot leave the nest to collect fresh food. The queen constantly alters the mouth of her nectar pot; when it contains only a little nectar it is left wide open, but when it is full it is often very nearly closed.

Brood development

In summer light, they range the woods, the lawns,
They sip the purple flowers, they skim the streams;
Soon urged by strange emotion of delight
To cherish nest and young.

Virgil, *Georgics*

When the tiny, white larvae hatch from the eggs they immediately start to feed on the pollen lump on which they find themselves. The queen now has to provide nectar and pollen for her larvae as well as for herself.

18

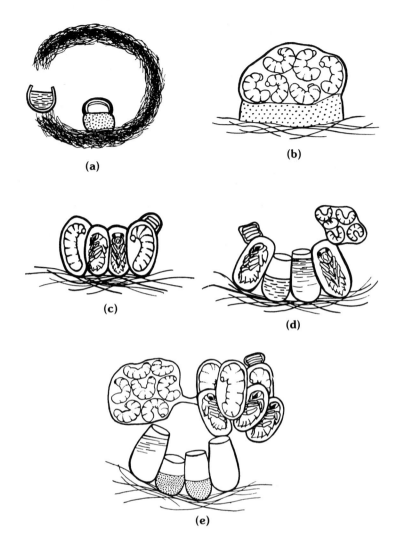

Figure 2.2 Cross sections of comb showing initial stages in the founding of a bumblebee colony (after Free & Butler). (a) The nest cavity: the honeypot is near the nest entrance. The eggs are contained in a wax chamber and rest on a lump of pollen (stippled). (b) The eggs have hatched into larvae. (c) The larvae have spun their cocoons and changed into pupae (in the inside cocoons) and prepupae (in the outside cocoons). A second batch of eggs has been laid on top of the right-hand cocoon. (d) Adult bees have emerged from the central cocoons of the first brood batch. The vacated cocoons are used for storing honey and pollen. (e) The comb grows upwards and outwards as new batches of brood are produced.

This she does by making temporary breaches in the wall of their wax canopy with her mandibles through which, with rapid contractions of her abdomen, she regurgitates the food from her honey-stomach. The queens of some species regurgitate into the larval cell a mixture of nectar and pollen, while those of others regurgitate nectar only into the cell and plaster pollen under each side of it so that the larvae lie on a cushion of pollen and take it directly for themselves.

As the larvae grow the queen incorporates more wax into the walls of their cells, so they still remain fully covered. In the later stages of their development the positions of the individual larvae, which lie curled on their sides, are evident as bulges in the wall of their wax covering.

When fully grown the larvae cease to feed, and each spins a silken cocoon round itself and adopts a more or less upright position. Until this stage of their life history none of the larvae have voided any faeces

19

Figure 2.3 Clump of bumblebee larvae. The wax covering has been removed.

which would, of course, foul the inside of the cell and also their food. However, once the cocoon is being constructed the larva's previously blocked hindgut opens to the exterior and it voids its accumulated faeces, before changing into a pupa. The faeces become spread over the inside of the cocoon and help to provide extra strength to its walls.

Once her larvae have changed into pupae the queen bumblebee removes the wax covering the yellow paper-like cocoons, and uses it to build more egg cells on top of some of them; all egg cells except the first are built on top of cocoons.

Figure 2.4 Bumblebee cocoons. The side wall of the centre cocoon has been removed to show the pupa inside.

While her first brood is developing the queen spends much time in her nest incubating it. She lies stretched over the brood clump, usually facing the nectar pot and nest entrance, and produces warmth by rapidly pulsating her thorax and abdomen. Her hairy dorsal surface acts as an insulating layer, and most of the warmth produced is transferred through her relatively hairless ventral surface to the brood and is sufficient to maintain them at 30–32 °C. However, as a queen is often away from her nest collecting food for 2 h or more at a time, the brood must be able to survive for some time without incubation.

As the larvae grow and the brood clump becomes larger the queen becomes unable to cover it all, and lies across its centre with her legs outstretched and her body flattened out to its fullest extent. This results in the larvae at the centre of the brood clump becoming lower than those at the sides, and thus a groove is formed in which the queen lies. This incubation groove becomes very obvious when the larvae have turned into pupae. At the end of the pupal stage the adults from cocoons in the centre of the groove are always the first to emerge; this is partly because the first eggs to be laid are in the centre of the original pollen lump, and partly because brood in the centre receive more warmth from the queen's body and are able to complete their development earlier than those at the periphery.

Indeed, differences in temperature as well as in the quantity and quality of food supply greatly influence the duration of a bumblebee's development. Within a single species the egg stage varies from 4 to 6 days, the larval stage from 10 to 19 days and the pupal stage from 10 to 18 days; hence in some circumstances the time from when an egg is laid

Figure 2.5 A worker bumblebee emerging from its cocoon.

until an adult is produced may be little over 3 weeks; in others it may be in excess of 6 weeks.

Usually all the first batch of bees produced are workers. When ready to emerge from its cocoon the young worker bee gnaws its way through the top of it, often being helped to do so by the queen, until it is able to push back the top of the cocoon as a circular flap and crawl out. At first the newly emerged bee appears very weak and unsteady; its silvery grey coat is soft and damp and its wings lie limply along its back. However, during the next day or so it steadily gains in strength; its coat dries and takes on the colour pattern typical of its species; its wings harden and become functional.

Most workers derived from the first egg batch emerge within a few days of each other. When they have done so they soon begin to perform tasks, including wax secretion, building and feeding the brood, previously done by the queen alone, so that a truly social unit in which a few workers and their mother co-operate for the common good becomes a reality.

Colony growth

> The prescient female rears her tender brood
> In strict proportion to the hoarded food.
>
> John Evans, 'The Bees'

Within a few days of their emergence some of the workers begin to forage and thereafter the queen remains in the comparative safety of her nest. However, in contrast to the queen honeybee, the queen bumble-bee continues to help her workers feed and incubate the brood and perform other tasks within the nest.

The egg cells that the queen built on top of her first batch of cocoons were slightly on the outer sides of them, so they did not get in the way of the young bees as they were emerging. When ready to lay eggs the queen inserts her abdomen into an egg cell and grips its sides and the surrounding part of the cocoon with her legs; the actual laying of each egg is accompanied by abdominal contractions while the queen either protrudes her sting over the brim of the egg cell, or thrusts it through the cell wall. After laying her eggs, which number between four and sixteen, the queen rapidly seals over the cell with wax.

Although eggs of the first batch are always laid on a bed of pollen, those of subsequent batches are usually laid so they come to lie in horizontal positions directly on the floor of the wax egg cells. A few species 'prime' all their egg cells with pollen; this habit recalls that of the more primitive solitary bees which 'mass provision' their larvae. However, this pollen is insufficient for bumblebee larvae to complete their

22

development, and in common with all bumblebee species the larvae are fed 'progressively' with nectar and pollen.

Soon after the queen's second batch of eggs has hatched, the workers produced from the first batch are ready to help their mother to look after the new larvae. When, in turn, these larvae pupate, more egg cells are built on top of their cocoons, with the result that the comb expands in a somewhat irregular way both upwards and outwards. These later batches of cocoons differ from the first in that they have no incubation grooves; indeed the larvae and pupae in the centre of a batch are usually higher than those at the periphery.

As a colony increases in size so does the rate at which its queen lays eggs, until she may lay a batch daily. Furthermore, the actual number of eggs that a queen lays in a cell tends to increase as a colony grows and is proportional to the number of cocoons in the batch on top of which it is built. Thus the number of eggs laid is adjusted to suit the number of workers that will be available to care for the larvae that hatch from them, and so the balance between the number of workers and the amount of brood is maintained.

The empty cocoons from which bumblebee workers have emerged are used for food storage; the jagged edges left by the emerging bees are trimmed and the heights and capacities of the cocoons are often increased by building up their walls with rings of wax. When filled with nectar they may be completely sealed over with wax. In some nests, cells constructed entirely of wax are also used for nectar storage; they are usually situated on the periphery of the comb.

Figure 2.6 Bumblebee cells for storing honey and pollen. The top central cell has just received pollen loads from a forager.

Figure 2.7 A *Bombus lucorum* colony. The older larvae, near the top of the comb, have become separated from each other.

Some species also store pollen in empty cocoons; these may be extended until they form tall wax cylinders up to 100 mm tall. These pollen storage cells mostly occur near the centre of the comb. Species that store their pollen in this way are known as 'pollen storers'.

Other species, known as 'pocket makers', place the pollen they have collected into special wax pouches or pockets which they build on to the outside of each group of larvae. The group expands over the pollen and the larvae feed directly on it. In addition, the larvae of such a group may also feed on pollen that, together with nectar, is regurgitated to them from time to time by the workers. In contrast, larvae of pollen-storing species are fed entirely on regurgitated pollen and nectar.

Because, in a pocket-making species, all the larvae produced from the eggs laid in a single batch feed on the same bed of pollen, they tend to remain in a compact group. Consequently, successive batches of brood are easily differentiated, and the whole comb has an orderly appearance. However, individual larvae of some pollen-storing species soon become separated, and occupy individual compartments or 'cells', and the relationship between them is no longer evident. In some pollen-storing species, small openings are left at the tops of the larval cells, a condition approaching that found in honeybees in which the cells remain open until shortly before the larvae are ready to pupate.

Division of labour

For where's the state beneath the firmament
That doth excel the bees for government.
Guillaume de Sallustre, 'Divine Weeks and Works'

Within a bumblebee colony there is great variation in worker size, and particularly so for pocket-making species. This is because of differences in the amount of food they received when larvae. When larvae of the pocket-making species enter their fourth and final instar, which is when they grow most rapidly, each spins a flimsy silken partition so that their positions relative to other larvae in the group become fixed. Some of the larvae in the group are in a better location to obtain food than others. Consequently they grow more rapidly and in doing so push those less favourably placed still further from the best locations. When the larvae pupate, some of the group will be much larger than others, and this is reflected in the size of the resulting adults. Badly undernourished larvae, from the periphery of the brood batch, often produce tiny adults with crippled wings. Because there is no direct competition between larvae of pollen-storing species, there is less variation in size of adults produced from the same egg batch; however, such variation as does exist can probably also be attributed to differences in the amount of food received by individual larvae. In the colonies of some species, but not others, there is evidence that the average size of the bumblebees produced in a nest increases as food becomes more abundant.

The size of an individual worker has an important influence on the tasks it undertakes. Like the honeybee, bumblebee workers tend first to do household duties and later to become foragers. However, the age at which a bumblebee starts to forage depends entirely on its size, and large workers begin foraging at an earlier age than smaller ones. When small workers do forage they do so less often than the larger ones. Hence on any one day, the average size of foragers is greater than that of house-bees.

There are two obvious advantages to this division of labour based on size. First, smaller bees are undoubtedly able to move through the narrow complex passages in a bumblebee comb with greater ease than larger bees, and secondly, the larger bees, which spend more of their lives foraging, can collect larger nectar and pollen loads and suck up nectar more quickly than the smaller bees. However, this division of labour is very adaptable to the needs of the colony and if the need arises house-bees will forage much earlier in their lives than usual, and similarly workers that have been foraging for some days will, if necessary, revert to house duties.

The size of a forager also governs to some extent whether it collects pollen or nectar only; larger foragers collect pollen on proportionally more trips than smaller foragers. However, the type of forage collected is primarily determined by the availability of nectar and pollen in the flowers, and the requirements of the colony. The requirements of the colony vary according to the relative abundance of its nectar and pollen stores and with the abundance of larvae which stimulate pollen col- 25

Figure 2.8 Bumblebee, *Bombus pascuolum*, collecting nectar from *Aubrieta deltoide* flowers.

lection. When a laden forager returns home it often appears very fastidious in the choice of cell in which to deposit its load, and may take some time selecting a suitable one. Possibly during its search the bee becomes 'aware' of the food requirements of its colony.

Having found a suitable cell or larval pocket in which to place its pollen, a pollen gatherer stands on the edge facing outward, holds both its rear legs over the cell, then by quick slicing movements of the middle pair of legs pushes pollen out of the pollen baskets and into the cell. Having unloaded its pollen a forager may use its mandibles to smooth the pollen down into the cell, or it may depart and leave the task to be done by a nest bee; individual bees vary in their behaviour at different times.

When discharging a nectar load a bee inserts its head into the honey-pot it has chosen, then with rapid contractions of its abdomen forces nectar from its honey-stomach and into the honeypot. During the course of a day, several of the honeypots in large nests may be filled in turn, but for small colonies there is a tendency for foragers to deposit their loads in only a limited number of the available honeypots, individual bees remaining fairly constant to one or two, although the choice appears to vary every few days.

Colony defence

Full merrily the humble-bee doth sing,
Till he hath lost his honey and his sting;
And being once subdued in armed tail,
Sweet honey and sweet notes together fail.

William Shakespeare, *Troilus and Cressida*

Bumblebees are attacked, both as adults and brood, by predators and parasites of various kinds. Other animals, including badgers and skunks, feed on the food stored in their combs, and even on the combs themselves, and many others act as scavengers and feed on the waste substances of the bumblebee colonies. It is not suprising therefore that apart from household and foraging duties some workers of large bumblebee colonies guard their nest. They stand inside the nest entrance and rapidly examine incoming bees with their antennae. When their nest is disturbed they buzz violently and often adopt a typical defensive posture, rolling over on their backs with the middle and hind leg on one side raised; returning foragers hesitate to pass them. All the members of a bumblebee colony share a common odour, which arises by absorption on their body surfaces of the combined odours of their combs, food and nest material, so that the guards are able to distinguish any intruder bumblebees from members of their own colony.

Probably guard duty is only undertaken when there are already enough bees doing the more important household and foraging duties. However, in small colonies which have no obvious guards some individuals more readily defend their colonies than others.

Climax of colony development

> The busy bee has no time for sorrow.
>
> William Blake, 'Proverbs of Hell'

The number of workers produced in a colony varies with the species. A thriving colony of a prolific species will rear 300–400 workers during the season, whereas those of others rarely produce as many as 100. Variations also occur within the same species even in the same year, and are partly due to variation in the fertility of the foundress queens and partly to local conditions.

The size attained by a bumblebee comb varies both within and between species: some may be barely 80 mm diameter, while others may attain 230 mm. The comb of a surface-nesting colony is nearly always approximately circular, whereas that in an underground nest often has to conform to the shape of the nest cavity. When the underground cavity is small the comb may even extend a little along the entrance tunnel, and old empty cocoons at the bottom of a comb are torn down to provide additional space. Fragments of broken cocoons are sometimes woven into the nest material.

As a colony grows the original nesting material often becomes inadequate to cover its expanding comb. Surface-nesting species are often able to add new material from the immediate vicinity; colonies nesting

27

underground at the end of tunnels are unable to do so, although they often build small 'pseudo-nests', composed of grass, moss or suitable debris, around the external openings of the nest tunnels.

When approaching full size, many colonies build canopies of wax over their combs. A canopy is attached to the sides of the comb and supported above it by wax pillars at various points. Sufficient space separates the canopy from the comb for the bees to be able to move freely. Canopies are much more commonly built by species which habitually nest underground than by those which nest on the surface, and their presence probably compensates for the smaller amount of nesting material available to underground colonies.

All the adults in a bumblebee colony incubate the brood, so much of the nectar collected is metabolised to produce heat; the nesting material and the wax canopy which surround a comb help to retain it. Bumblebees also prevent their colonies from becoming too hot; they do this by using their wings to fan currents of cooler air over their combs, and by making temporary openings in their nest covering. These regulatory activities can be remarkably efficient and, although the temperature of a developing colony is subject to fluctuation, that of a mature colony remains near to 30 °C.

Production of males and queens

Their young succession all their cares employ.

Virgil, *Georgics*

Stability of colony temperature undoubtedly favours the production of males and queens, which occurs at the maturity or 'climax' of the colony. Some colonies produce males only, some queens only, some both males and queens and some, of course, succumb before they can produce either.

Male bumblebees are produced from unfertilised eggs. They are always reared in a colony before any queens are produced. A male can be distinguished from workers or queens by the absence of a sting, the presence of a copulatory apparatus ('claspers') on the tip of his abdomen, the presence of an extra overlapping cuticular plate covering the dorsal surface of his abdomen, making 13 altogether, and antennae that are proportionately longer. In addition, the males of some species can readily be distinguished from the workers and queens by differences in their external colour markings.

Both queens and workers are produced from fertilised eggs. The queens are usually larger than workers of the same species, but there are no other external distinguishing features. The difference in size between

28

queens and workers is clearly marked in some of the pollen-storing species but not in others; and in some pocket-making species there are no distinct differences in size between the two castes. The only essential differences between workers and queens are physiological. For example, queens live much longer than workers and alone are able to survive the winter due to their ability, not shared by workers, to develop their fat bodies.

Although queens need to hibernate before their ovaries develop, the ovaries of worker bumblebees, which usually remain as undifferentiated threads, may develop under certain circumstances and the workers may build egg cells and lay unfertilised eggs. This occurs most frequently at the climax of colony development, when the first males and queens are emerging. It seems that a relatively large worker population, a reduction in the amount of work to be done in the colony, an abundance of food, and a stable and relatively high temperature combine to facilitate ovary development in worker bumblebees.

When egg-laying workers are present in a colony the usual state of harmony is lost; the queen is hostile to such workers and often attempts to eat any eggs they lay, and the workers often attack each other. Should the mother of a colony die, one of the workers appears to adopt her status; this dominant worker spends most of its time astride a new egg cell in which it has laid eggs, and butts its head against any worker that comes too near. Sometimes there is a simple form of hierarchical organisation which is based solely on the dominance of one or more bees over the others. However, while the mother queen is present, her dominating and policing activities help prevent most of the workers from laying eggs and so help maintain the stability and cohesion of the colony. As we shall see later, in the honeybee colony this physical dominance has evolved into a more subtle and more effective dominance by chemical messages.

It is not known for certain why a colony ceases to rear workers in favour of males and queens, but it seems that queen production is mostly controlled by the quantity of food given to the larvae. It is supposed that larvae that give rise to workers are inadequately nourished, whereas at the climax of colony development, when queens are produced, there are more workers and food is more plentiful than before, and each female larva receives enough food and attention to develop into a queen. Unlike honeybee queen larvae, those bumblebee larvae destined to become queens do not appear to receive any special glandular food.

Various factors may contribute to this increased nourishment of the larvae that permits queen production. The egg-laying rate of the mother queen sometimes diminishes markedly prior to the production of sexual forms, and this, of course, results in an increase in the number of

29

workers available to care for each of the larvae present. The effect of this increase in the larva:worker ratio is reinforced in some species by adult workers actually destroying some of the eggs and larvae. Some colonies contain fewer workers than others of the same species at the time queens are produced. Probably these colonies are located where the supply of forage is particularly abundant and accessible.

It appears that in pocket-making species the diet of larvae destined to become queens is supplemented with pollen regurgitated to them by workers, so the usual competition between larvae of the same batch is diminished, and all receive sufficient food to develop into queens. The sharp distinction between the sizes of the workers and queens of pollen-storing species probably reflects the absence of any direct competition for food between the larvae which occupy individual cells early in development.

Mating behaviour

> Drones that laugh at honest toil, and reap
> Where others sowed.
>
> Virgil, *Georgics*

Most male bumblebees leave their nests when about 2–4 days old and, unlike male honeybees, most never return to them again, but forage to satisfy their needs. While in their nests they serve no useful purpose apart from incubating the brood. In contrast, young queens usually first leave their maternal nest later in life than males, and frequently collect nectar and pollen for their maternal colony, as well as performing various tasks in the nest, including feeding the brood, producing wax and defending the colony. However, at this stage the important function of a queen is to mate and prepare herself for hibernation.

During copulation the male mounts upon the back of the female and with his claspers grips the tip of his abdomen to that of the queen. Copulation can often readily be induced merely by confining young queens and males together in a small container. However, as with many other activities, different species of bumblebee differ widely in their mating habits. Males of some species lie in wait for a passing queen; each remains close to a prominent object, such as a flower, fence post or rock, sometimes hovering in the air above it and sometimes standing still and very alert with antennae held erect and wings half spread ready to dart after any likely looking insect that passes by. Although the males of species that exhibit this habit have very large eyes, it seems that they can only recognise a queen when very close. If the insect that he chased proves to be a queen of his own species, the male will attempt to mate.

Figure 2.9 Bumblebee
(Bombus pratorum)
male (left) mating with
young queen.

Otherwise he will return to his observation post. Males of other species congregate around the entrances of nests of their own species and, when young queens appear, attempt to seize them and mate; sometimes they chase the queens into the nest entrance and perhaps mate with them in the nest itself.

However, the most interesting behaviour is shown by the males of certain species which fly, in a seemingly endless procession, along established flight circuits to which queens are attracted and mating occurs. Special visiting places, which may range from an area at the base of a tree or shrub to a small twig or single leaf, occur along the circuits. The circumference of an individual flight route is about 300 m and consists of numerous visiting places varying from less than a metre to about 18 m apart. Although each male follows his own particular circuit, the circuits of different males overlap, and several visiting places are held in common, so that in a given area there is a network of interwoven routes along which the males fly in all directions. However, the flight routes of individual males are not static, but vary slightly from day to day, certain visiting places along them being discarded and others incorporated.

At the beginning of each day, males scent-mark their visiting places with an odour produced by the label glands in their heads. When doing so they grip with their mandibles the leaves, twigs or pieces of bark which they are scent-marking and make gnawing movements, often simultaneously whirring their wings. The scents used to mark the flight routes are characteristic of the species, and this partly explains why only members of the same species use the same visiting places. The

31

tendency of different species to establish their flight routes at different heights above the ground also helps to avoid interspecific mating. Males of one group regularly fly at tree-top level, those of another at the level of bushes or shrubs, another at the level of herbage, and those of a final group have flight paths nearly at ground level. Even within the same locality there may be noticeable differences in the levels at which males of the different species fly. However, the behaviour of the males is adaptable; for example, species whose flightpaths are normally at tree-top level will, in treeless regions, use routes closer to the ground.

Males are readily attracted to queens near the visiting places and there can be little doubt that a queen entering the mosaic of flight routes soon becomes mated.

While the young queen remains attached to her maternal colony she frequently helps herself to the stored food, and the size of her fat bodies increases greatly to form her food reserves during hibernation; eventually she fills her honey-stomach, leaves her maternal nest and goes into hibernation. Queens of some species enter hibernation while it is still the height of summer.

Bumblebee queens hibernate in separate spherical chambers, about 30 mm wide, which they excavate for themselves at 2–15 cm below the level of the soil. The hibernation sites selected are always well drained. Banks facing north or north-west are commonly chosen; queens hibernating in banks with these aspects are unlikely to be roused prematurely by the warmth of the winter sun. Some species prefer to hibernate at the base of trees where leaf litter accumulates.

Colony decline

There's a whisper down the field where the year has shot her yield,
And the ricks stand grey to the sun
Singing: 'Over then, come over, for the bee has quit the clover,
And your English summer's done'.

Rudyard Kipling, 'The Long Trail'

After males and queens are produced a colony never rears any new worker brood, although the spermatheca (sperm storage sac) of the old queen may still contain an ample supply of sperm. As the old workers die there is a steady decline in the colony population, and after the last adult males and queens have emerged and departed, the queen and few remaining workers, all looking rather tattered and shiny where the hair has rubbed off their bodies, spend most of their time resting idly on top of the comb. They no longer maintain the nest temperature at its previous level, and when they die, decay and parasites soon destroy the comb.

Oh, for a bee's experience
Of clover and of noon.

Emily Dickinson

The relationship between bees and flowers has been the source of much fascination ever since Christian Konrad Sprengel first drew attention to the great many flower species that depend upon insects to pollinate them.

It is well known that flowers of irregular shape, in contrast to ones that are radially symmetrical, are particularly favoured by bumblebees and have become known as 'bumblebee' flowers. Even so, different species of bumblebee often prefer different flower species. Preference appears to be associated with the depth of the flowers' corolla tubes, the length of the bees' tongues and the bees' preferences for foraging in different sorts of places. For example, whereas some species visit flowers in exposed places such as open fields, moorland or the tops of hedges and high trees, others may restrict their foraging mainly to sheltered situations such as hedge-bottoms, gardens, thickets or other sites with tall dense vegetation.

Because many species of bumblebee have long tongues that are able to reach the nectar at the base of deep-throated flowers, and because they have justly gained the reputation of continuing to work in the field under conditions in which honeybees stay at home, they have become recognised as valuable pollinators of many of our agricultural crops.

In his *Origin of Species*, published in 1859, Charles Darwin reported that 100 heads of red clover that were visited by bumblebees produced 2700 seeds whereas another 100 heads that had been protected from visiting bees produced none! Yet only 40 years earlier a beekeeper had suggested that bumblebees should be destroyed because they competed with his honeybee colonies for forage, and added: 'I consider the finding of a Bumble Bee's nest as no mean Treasure, for as they are like the common bee great hoarders of honey, I always rob them of their labour, and give it to my bees, who banquet on it with truly epicurean gluttony'.

Although it is now recognised that the bumblebee is one of the most efficient pollinating insects in the world, it is generally agreed that bumblebees are usually too few for adequate pollination, and even in those areas where they abound in some years they are relatively scarce in others.

It is commonly supposed that the bumblebee population, in common with those of the solitary bees, has declined in recent years, and some authorities have suggested that this has diminished the amount of seed produced by certain cultivated crops. A number of reasons have been given to account for this.

Modern methods of intensive cultivation tend to destroy hedgerows, banks and rough ground, and so reduce the number of nests and nesting sites. The use of herbicides on farm crops and on verges destroys plants, often before they flower, on which the bees forage; and the use of insecticides can destroy the wild bees themselves.

However, although it is likely that there has been a decrease in the number of wild bees in Europe and North America during the last few decades, it is extremely difficult to demonstrate that any such change has occurred, and it is only in a few areas where agriculture and pesticides are being introduced for the first time that this has been possible. Furthermore, it must be remembered that changes in the popularity and economic value of flowering crops, and an enlightened use of roadside verges, particularly the wide verges of motorways, to produce an abundance of flowering herbs, shrubs and trees, can quickly help to redress the balance.

We have briefly discussed the possibility of introducing beneficial species of solitary bee into parts of the world where they do not already occur in order to take advantage of their pollinating abilities. Similar benefits could result from introducing bumblebees. In fact, bumblebees were introduced from Britain into New Zealand toward the end of the last century. The first successful attempts were made by the Canterbury Acclimatisation Society in 1885 and 1886, when 93 out of a total of 442 queens survived the sea passage. In less than 10 years the progeny from these queens had spread throughout New Zealand and it was reported that the seed crop from red clover had increased considerably.

However, importation of a foreign species should never be undertaken lightly. There may be a chance that they are carrying disease or parasites that are absent in the host country. Furthermore, when the pollinating insect is removed from its natural environment and the flower species to which it has become adapted during the course of evolution it may cease to be useful, because when a flower and a foraging insect are not well adapted to each other, insect visits may occur without accompanying pollination. This occurs when certain species of bumblebee, that have relatively short tongues, visit flowers with long corolla tubes and cannot reach the nectar by entering the flowers in the normal way. Instead they make holes by biting through the corolla, near its base, with their mandibles, and through these holes they can insert their tongues into the nectaries, and so obtain nectar without pollinating.

No doubt the characteristic differences in tongue length between different bumblebee species help to explain their differences in foraging preferences. But even when two bumblebee colonies of the same species are located side by side they may differ in the way in which they exploit the surrounding flora; this indicates some type of communication within the colony. *Bumblebee foraging*

The inhabitants of a bumblebee colony take little notice of foragers that have just returned home, although they may occasionally nibble at any pollen they are carrying, and if nectar is in short supply many of them drink some of it as soon as it has been discharged into a honeypot. Only rarely does one bumblebee pass food directly to another. Although the eager way in which a forager that has just returned home searches for a suitable receptacle in which to deposit its load may perhaps excite other members of a colony to leave the nest and search for food, particularly at the beginning of a day, it is well established that bumblebees cannot communicate the location of a source of food directly to other members of their colony.

It seems that the odour of the predominant stores of nectar and pollen in a nest induces foragers to seek the flowers from which they were collected. Chance differences in the food collected by two colonies would soon become magnified, and could account for their different foraging preferences. The foragers of honeybee colonies are also influenced by this simple and indirect form of communication, although, as we shall see later, there is superimposed upon it one of the most complex and fascinating forms of communication in the animal kingdom.

Part II

Honeybees

. . . for so work the honey-bees,
Creatures that by a rule in nature, teach
The art of order to a peopled kingdom.
They have a king, and officers of sorts:
Where some, like magistrates, correct at home;
Others, like merchants, venture trade abroad;
Others, like soldiers, armed in their stings,
Make boot upon the summer's velvet buds;
Which pillage they with merry march bring home
To the tent-royal of their emperor:
Who, busied in his majesty, surveys
The singing masons building roofs of gold;
The civil citizens kneading-up the honey;
The poor mechanic porters crowding in
Their heavy burdens at his narrow gate;
The sad-eyed justice, with his surly hum,
Delivering o'er to executors pale
The lazy yawning drone. . . .
                    William Shakespeare, *King Henry V*

3 *True honeybees*

Species and evolution

The true honeybees belong to the genus *Apis*. The most well known and most widely distributed species is *Apis mellifera*. It extends throughout the temperate zone as well as to parts of the Tropics and sub-Arctic. It is native to Africa, Europe and western Asia and was taken by pioneers into North and South America and Australasia, where some of the largest yields of honey are produced.

There are three other species of honeybee, all of which are confined to southeastern Asia. *Apis cerana* resembles *Apis mellifera* in building a series of combs and in nesting in sheltered cavities; both these species can be kept in hives. It is generally assumed that the behaviour of *Apis cerana* resembles that of *Apis mellifera*. Because *Apis mellifera* is a superior honey producer, it has been introduced by man into some regions previously occupied exclusively by *Apis cerana*.

The other two species – *Apis dorsata*, the giant honeybee, and *Apis florea*, the dwarf honeybee – each build only a single comb suspended from tree branches, ledges and cliffs in the open, as well as from the rooves of caves. Whereas the comb of the dwarf honeybee is often no larger than the size of a man's hand, the comb of the giant honeybee can

Figure 3.1 Comb of honeybee, *Apis cerana*.

Figure 3.2 Colony of honeybee, *Apis dorsata*, near Poona, India, showing single comb covered with bees.

Figure 3.3 Colonies of honeybee, *Apis dorsata*, suspended from branches of a tree, near Bangalore, India.

be as much as 2 m long by 1 m deep. These two species are not kept in hives, but are hunted extensively.

Although the colony organisation of the giant and dwarf honeybees obviously resembles in many ways that of *Apis mellifera*, we know far too little about their biology, and so this account will concern itself with *Apis mellifera*.

40

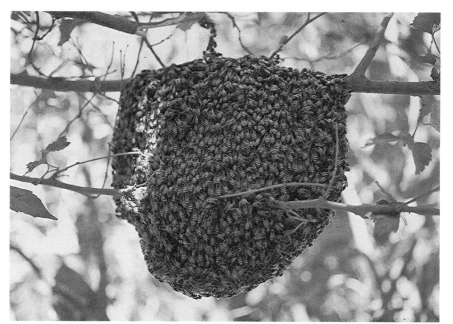

Figure 3.4 The single comb of a colony of the dwarf honeybee, *Apis florea*, North India.

Figure 3.5 Queen and attendant workers of *Apis florea* honeybee colony.

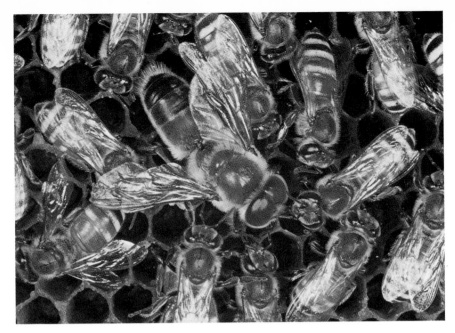

Figure 3.6 A drone and workers from an *Apis florea* honeybee colony.

Composition of the colony

> That wooden hive between the trees
> Is Palace of a Queen – of Bees.
> With seed-black eyes, and hidden stings
> Sentries, at entry, beat their wings
> To cool the night-dark gallery
> Where waxen-celled Princesses lie;
> And drones – their grubs – sleep snug near by,
> While busier bees store honey!
>
> Walter de la Mare, 'The Garden'

Each colony of the honeybee *(Apis mellifera)* consists of a single fertile female, who is the mother of the colony and is commonly known as the 'queen', several thousand sterile females known as 'workers', and at certain times of the year up to several hundred male bees known as 'drones'.

Under natural conditions, the home of the colony is a hollow tree or cave where it builds itself a series of parallel wax combs, about 10 mm apart, each comb having a single layer of horizontal hexagonal cells on either side. In these beautifully executed cells the food is stored and the young are reared.

THE QUEEN

> And for their monarch Queen – an egg-casting machine,
> Helpless without attendance as a farmer's drill.
>
> Robert Bridges, 'The Testament of Beauty'

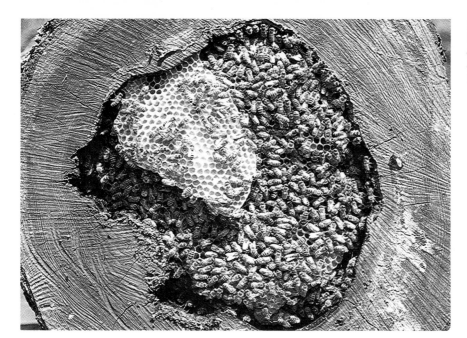

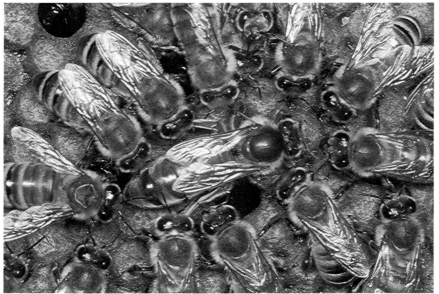

Figure 3.8 Queen honeybee *(Apis mellifera)* and her 'court' of workers.

During the course of evolution the queen has become specialised as the producer of eggs and is strikingly different in appearance from her workers. Her ovaries are so well developed that her abdomen has become greatly distended and she may lay as many as 2000 eggs per day. Unlike the bumblebee queen, she has lost the ability to feed her young, produce wax, build comb or gather nectar and pollen. Indeed, a mature honeybee queen no longer feeds herself but is entirely dependent upon the workers for her food.

43

The queen spends her time moving over the combs, inspecting cells and laying eggs in those that are empty and prepared to receive them. She lays two types of egg, fertilised and unfertilised. The fertilised eggs give rise to workers or queens, and the unfertilised give rise to drones.

When a queen mates she receives enough sperm to last the rest of her life, and this is stored in a special sac, the spermatheca, in her abdomen. Sperm are released from the spermatheca to fertilise eggs as they are about to be laid. Drones are reared in larger cells than workers; before the queen lays in a cell, she is able to determine by its characteristic odour, and its size, which she 'measures' with her front pair of legs, whether it should receive a fertilised or an unfertilised egg.

THE DRONES

> From the Lime's leaf no amber drops they steal,
> Nor bear their grooveless thighs the foodful meal;
> On other's toils, in pamper'd leisure, thrive
> The lazy Fathers of th' industrious hive.
>
> John Evans, 'The Bees'

Drones are produced in most honeybee colonies from May to July. The drone lacks the food-gathering apparatus of the worker but has very large eyes and long antennae, which he uses to locate the queen during mating flights. Indeed drones have no function other than that of mating with the queens.

Figure 3.9 A drone honeybee being evicted from its hive by workers.

Drones are not permanent residents of the colony and, towards the end of the season, when less forage is being collected, they are no longer reared and those already present are herded into a corner of the hive. Eventually chilled and almost moribund, they are dragged from the hive entrance by the workers.

THE WORKERS

All we need is to be industrious not like a machine but like the honeybee.
                                                                Mahatma Gandhi

We have seen that queens cannot survive without the workers; workers can survive but cannot increase in numbers without queens. In fact, apart from laying fertile eggs, all the tasks which are necessary for the growth and survival of the colony are done by the workers. During their lives, which may be of only 4–6 weeks' duration in mid-summer but several months in the winter, each worker bee usually undertakes a variety of tasks which are, in general, linked with its age and physiological condition, although there is no rigid demarcation as to when one task ends and another begins.

These tasks include feeding and caring for the brood produced from the queen's eggs, building new comb and repairing existing comb, defending the colony and foraging for food, water and propolis, which is a resinous exudate from the buds or bark of various trees.

To perform these tasks their bodies possess a number of specialised features which are absent in the queen. These features will be described as we discuss the activities of the workers in more detail.

Development of the brood

They breed, they brood, instruct and educate,
And make provision for the future state:
They work their waxen lodgings in the hives,
And labour honey to sustain their lives.

                                                                Virgil, *Georgics*

One bee is reared per cell from an egg that the queen lays upright on the cell base. After 3 days the movements of the embryo inside the egg cause the membranes to rupture and free it. Food is available on the cell base before or immediately after hatching and is supplied throughout larval development. It has been calculated that after 24 h a worker or queen larva is five times its weight at hatching, and this rate of increase continues every 24 h for the next 4 days! Thereafter the worker larva increases in weight at a slower rate.

45

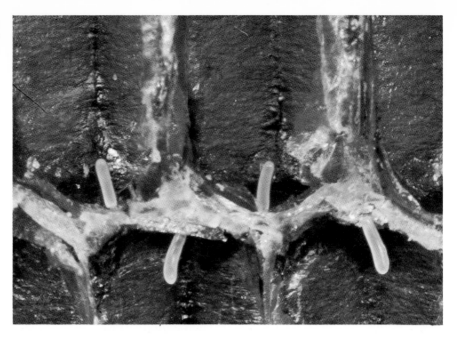

Figure 3.10 Section of honeybee comb showing eggs laid on the bases of the cells.

Figure 3.11 Cells of honeybee comb containing larvae.

Nearly all the activity of the larva is concerned with obtaining food and feeding. It lies curled in the base of its cell with its dorsal surface facing outwards, and uses its body folds or its sides and back as locomotory appendages.

After about 5 days for a queen or worker larva and 7 days for a drone

46

larva, no more food is provided and the cell is sealed with a capping of wax by adult worker bees. The larva uncurls along the length of its cell and proceeds to construct its cocoon. This is made of silk, from a single spinneret, applied to the inside surface of the cell.

Within 18 h of the beginning of cocoon construction the larva defaecates for the first time. While doing so, it continues somersaulting in its cell, applying the silk to the cell walls, and its faeces become incorporated into the cocoon. Their presence darkens and perhaps strengthens the cocoon, and helps account for the dark colour of comb in which several generations of bees have been reared.

The capping over the mouth of a cell is porous and rough, consisting of an aggregate of particles, in contrast to the cell walls and bases which are smooth and non-porous. The texture of the capping is important in enabling the larva to recognise and face the mouth of the cell when it has completed spinning its cocoon and is ready to enter the quiescent pupal stage. This ensures that when the adults appear (about 16 days after the egg has been laid for the queen, 21 for the worker, and 24 for the drone) they are facing the right direction to emerge.

When ready to emerge, the bee perforates the capping by removing bits of wax which it fastens to the wall just inside its cell. Older bees may also help by thinning down the cappings before emergence, or removing some of it during emergence. Eventually the perforations are large enough for the emerging bee to force its way out of the cell, the capping often being pushed back like a hinged lid when it does so.

Development of the brood

Figure 3.12 Section of honeybee comb showing pupae.

Figure 3.13 Worker honeybee emerging from its cell.

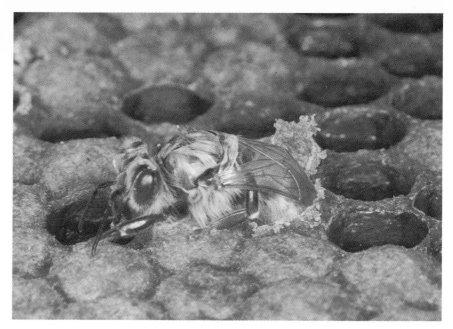

Workers' duties

Vast numbers throng'd the fruitful hive;
  Yet those vast numbers made 'em thrive;
Millions endeavouring to supply
  Each other's lust and vanity.

Bernard Mandeville, 'The Fable of the Bees'

When a worker bee emerges from its cell its cuticle is pale and still soft and takes a day or so to harden and acquire its full colouration. During this time it does little but clean cells ready to receive eggs and stored food. But it also receives nectar or honey from more mature bees and helps itself to the colony's honey and pollen stores. Honey is the colony's main carbohydrate source and pollen provides the fats and proteins. As a result of its ample food consumption certain physiological changes take place in the young bee, notable among which is the development of special glands in its head, known as the hypopharyngeal glands. These glands are a source of a secretion rich in fats and protein that the worker bee of a few days old is able to feed to developing brood.

Whereas larvae destined to grow into workers or drones are fed this special 'brood food' for the first 2–3 days of their development, and for the next 2–3 days are fed largely on a mixture of honey and pollen regurgitated directly to them by the workers, those larvae destined to become queens are fed brood food until they pupate. The brood is subject to continuous care and attention. It has been estimated that each larva

48

receives several hundred visits from nurse bees on each day, although of
course it is only fed on a small porportion of these.

The queen honeybee is also fed with the secretion from the workers' hypopharyngeal glands, and her egg-laying rate is controlled in large measure by the amount of it she is given by the workers. Indeed it would be impossible for her to achieve her regular production of several hundred eggs per day during favourable seasons without receiving large quantities of rich, quickly assimilated food.

At about the same time that a young worker bee has developed brood food glands, or a little later, it starts to produce wax. There are four pairs of wax glands opening on the lower surface of the abdomen. The wax issues as thin white translucent sheets which the bee removes with its third pair of legs and passes forward to the front pair of legs and mandibles where they are chewed and moulded into the comb.

The wax may be used to build new comb, it may be used to repair damaged comb, or it may be used to build a wax cap over the mouth of a cell containing honey or larvae that are ready to become pupae.

To produce wax bees need to consume large amounts of carbohydrate and long festoons of bees may often be seen hanging in parts of the nest where new comb is being built. Indeed, for much of its time in the nest a bee appears to be relatively inactive, and remains almost motionless. It could often be secreting wax or special food for the brood, but its appearance belies the common conception of being 'as busy as a bee'.

The hexagonal cells comprising the comb are of two basic types. The larger deeper ones (6.9 mm in diameter) are used for the rearing of drone brood, and the smaller ones (5.4 mm in diameter) for the rearing of worker brood. Although irregularly shaped cells are constructed where worker and drone cells adjoin and where combs are attached to their supports, it is a constant source of wonder as to how bees manage to produce these often flawless mosaics of hexagonal cells. This is especially so as the bees appear to work in a very unsystematic manner, and one bee may remove the wax that another has just added! As Karl Marx remarked: 'a bee puts to shame many an architect in the construction of her cells. But what distinguishes the worst architect from the best of bees is this, that the architect raises his structure in imagination before he erects it in reality'. We shall see later that the type of cell built, and whether it is used for food storage or brood rearing, varies at different times, and has important consequences for the colony's activities.

After a period of several days, or even 2–3 weeks spent tending the brood and secreting wax, the worker bee may move to the next stage of its sequence of duties and begin to pack down loads of pollen that the pollen gatherers have deposited in their cells, and to receive loads of nectar collected by foragers. Part of the alimentary canal at the front of

Figure 3.14 Transfer of food between two worker honeybees. The bee on the left, with its tongue extended, is receiving food from the bee on the right.

the abdomen of a worker bee is enlarged to form a honey-stomach in which nectar is collected and carried back to the nest. On returning home the successful nectar gatherer does not deposit this in a cell itself but gives it to bees that are still engaged in nest duties. The bee that is receiving food extends its tongue and pushes it between the mouth parts of the nectar gatherer who proceeds to regurgitate nectar from its honey-stomach. During the transfer of food the antennae of both bees are in constant contact and help them to keep orientated to each other. The antennae also have another function; their position serves as a signal as to when food transfer shall cease.

The bees that receive food from foragers do not themselves usually store it in the cells of the comb, but in turn pass it on to other bees. In fact, in a honeybee colony, food is often passed from one worker bee to another, and between bees of any age, although in general bees more often give food to those younger than themselves than to older bees. As a result, within a colony there is a tendency for food to pass from the older bees, which are foragers, to the younger bees, which are often engaged in feeding brood and producing wax, and so have the greatest carbohydrate need.

Orientation flights

Oft have I wondered at the faultless skill
With which thou trackest out thy dwelling cave,
Winging thy way with seeming careless will
From mount to plain, o'er lake and winding wave.

Thomas Smibert, 'To the Wild Bee'

When only a few days old bees make their first flights outside their nests. *Orientation flights* These first flights are of short duration. During them the bees are enabled to void their accumulated faeces, and to learn the location of their nest in relation to its surroundings.

Probably, bees are readily able to learn the location of their nest site in natural conditions where it is surrounded by a wealth of readily discernible features, and, with increase in the number of orientation flights as they grow older, they become skilled in locating their hive from some distance away and are unlikely to make mistakes. However, they are not infallible; when beekeepers put colonies into identical hives that are in close proximity and facing in the same direction, the bees often make mistakes and return to a hive other than their own.

Changes in the vegetation near a natural nest, or movement of a hive by a beekeeper, can cause even an experienced bee to search for the entrance on its return home.

Near the tip of its abdomen a worker bee has a special gland known after its discoverer as the Nasonov gland. The odour it produces is highly attractive to other bees. When a 'lost' bee does eventually succeed in locating its home it often stands at the entrance, faces in toward the nest, and elevates the tip of its abdomen and exposes its Nasonov gland. At the same time it fans with its wings and so wafts a current of air over the surface of the gland, aiding the dispersal of the odour. By doing so it helps to guide other searching bees back to their colony. This provides another example of how the behaviour of the individual is adapted to the needs of the colony as a whole.

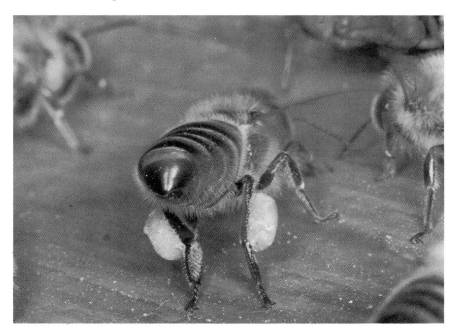

Figure 3.15 A pollen gatherer that has returned to its hive, fanning its wings and exposing its Nasonov gland, located near the tip of its abdomen. The odour from the gland attracts other bees.

True honeybees   An established honeybee colony always contains comb, food stores, propolis, adult workers and a queen. Odours from each of these facilitate nest recognition and induce a previously 'lost' bee to expose its Nasonov gland. However, the odour of brood, which is absent during part of the winter and other dearth periods, fails to do so.

Much of the communication between members of a honeybee colony is by chemical substance or 'messages' known in scientific circles as 'pheromones'. That produced by the Nasonov gland was the first honeybee pheromone to be discovered.

Colony defence

> Wise Nature has combined in the bee the sweetness of its honey with the sharpness of its sting.
>
> Baltasar Grecian, *Oraculo Manual*

Other activities frequently seen at the nest entrance are associated with its defence. The food stores of the honeybee colony are attractive to many potential robbers, including bees from other colonies. Between the time that bees receive loads of forage and themselves fly to the field to search for it, some bees become guards. They stand or patrol at the hive entrance, often for days in succession, and rapidly examine incoming bees with their antennae. All the bees belonging to the same colony share the same distinctive odour, and if a bee trying to enter a hive has a

Figure 3.16
A honeybee that has stung an intruder leaves its sting and part of its gut behind.

strange smell, and so belongs to a different colony, or if it behaves in a 'suspicious' manner, the guard bees bite and may even attempt to sting it. Guards are frequently to be seen poised, with their mandibles often slightly agape, and forelegs off the ground ready to pounce on any likely intruder.

An alert guard bee is also able to communicate alarm to its companions by releasing an odour (pheromone) from a gland in its sting chamber. When a bee attacks an intruder, such as a mammal or bird, its barbed sting becomes embedded in the soft flesh of its adversary, and when the bee tries to free itself the sting apparatus is severed at a predetermined breaking point and left behind, where it continues to pump poison into the intruder's flesh. At the same time the severed sting emits the alarm pheromone, which has the effect of guiding other guard bees to the target; hence the altruistic behaviour of the bee that stung, and in doing so forfeited its life, will not have been in vain. The defending bees often grip an intruder with their mandibles and mark it with another alarm pheromone produced from glands in their heads. Alarm pheromones tend to be very volatile, so their effect is not prolonged, and when danger has passed the colony soon returns to normal.

A honeybee worker sometimes strays to the hive entrance of another colony by mistake and when this happens it is examined carefully, without, however, being attacked. Probably in an attempt to appease the guards, the inadvertent intruder offers them a drop of regurgitated food. Although in a bumblebee nest no direct transfer of food occurs between one worker bumblebee and another, very occasionally when a bumblebee is attacked by a 'dominant' one it will offer its attacker a drop of food. It seems, therefore, that the transfer of food between worker honeybees, which plays such an important role in their social organisation, could well have evolved from an attacked bee's habit of offering food to its aggressor.

Foragers

> Blaw, blaw ye wastin' winds, blaw soft
> Amang the leafy trees,
> With gentle gale from hill and dale
> Bring hame the laden bees.
>
> Robert Burns, 'O' a' the airts'

During the latter part of their lives worker bees become foragers. They usually first leave their hives to forage when 2–4 weeks old, and once a bee has begun foraging it continues to do so for the rest of its life.

In addition to gathering nectar and pollen, some of the foragers of a colony may collect water, to dilute honey or cool their nest (see later), 53 and propolis, which they use for plugging small openings in the walls of their nest and reducing the size of large openings.

During a single foraging trip a bee may visit several hundred flowers to collect its load of nectar or pollen. On return home a nectar gatherer gives its load of nectar, carried in its honey-stomach, to one or more nest bees near the entrance. Inside the nest the load is passed from bee to bee and, eventually, it is converted into honey. This the bees accomplish by exposing the nectar as thin films on their tongues, to reduce its water content, and by adding the enzyme 'invertase' from their hypopharyngeal glands which changes the 'sucrose' sugar of nectar into the 'fructose' and 'glucose' sugars of honey.

Pollen readily collects on the branched hairs with which a bee's body is covered. The bees use their front legs to brush this pollen from their heads and bodies and transfer it to their rear legs where it is lodged in their special, concave outer surfaces known as 'pollen baskets' or 'corbiculae', which are fringed with long recurved hairs, and carried back to the nest.

Attraction to flowers

And then pell-mell his harvest follows swift,
    Blossom and borage, lime and balm and clover,
On Downs the thyme, on cliffs the scantling thrift,
    Everywhere bees go racing with the hours,
For every bee becomes a drunken lover,
    Standing upon his head to sup the flowers.

                V. Sackville-West, 'The Land'

Bees are attracted to flowers and recognise them by their colour, shape and scent. When working flowers of one colour only, they become conditioned to it and do not visit flowers of another colour. Bees are unable to distinguish red as a distinct colour, but they *are* able to perceive ultra-violet; so the flower colours seen by bees are not necessarily the same as those perceived by man.

However, scent is the most important means by which bees recognise flowers, and they readily learn to associate a particular kind of flower with a particular scent or mixture of scents. Although the general shape of a flower, and especially its colour, guide bees to it from a distance, when bees come close to a flower, scent provides the stimulus to alight. Indeed, a bee's threshold for scent perception is usually much lower than that of man, and honeybees and bumblebees can become conditioned to flowers that man cannot smell.

Nectar and pollen are, of course, the bait that flowers use to attract pollinators. The unfolding of the petals, scent production and nectar secretion are so timed that they coincide with the anthers producing mature pollen which the visiting foragers carry on their bodies to the flowers' stigmas. Soon after a flower is fertilised, and visits by pollinating bees are no longer needed, the petals wither and scent and nectar production ceases.

Collection of nectar and pollen

> The careful insect midst his works I view,
> Now from the flowers exhaust the fragrant dew,
> With golden treasures load his little thighs
> And steer his distant journey through the skies.
>
> John Gay, 'Rural Sports'

Honeybees visit some flower species for nectar only, a few for pollen only, but the vast majority for both nectar and pollen.

The nectaries may occur on many parts of the flower, including the petals, sepals and bases of the stamens and stigma. The amount and concentration of the nectar they secrete varies from one flower to another. It is obviously to a forager's advantage to collect from flowers producing abundant nectar of high sugar concentration, so some flower species are favoured over others. Foraging bees also have a greater inducement to fill their honey-stomachs to their maximum capacity (about 70 mg) with increase in the nectar's attractiveness. Indeed, when the sugar concentration of nectar is below a certain level the relatively large amount of energy needed to evaporate its water content to produce honey may make its collection uneconomical.

Figure 3.17
A honeybee gathering pollen and nectar from oil seed rape (*Brassica napus*).

However, even within a single flower species, the sugar concentration of the nectar may differ considerably at different times of the day and in different weather conditions, and as a result the attractiveness of many flower species to honeybees varies accordingly. This especially applies to shallow open flowers whose nectaries are more exposed to fluctuations in wind, temperature and relative humidity.

Some flower species also exhibit a characteristic daily rhythm of nectar secretion which is closely followed by the abundance of nectar-gathering bees visiting it. So closely do some bees become conditioned to the time of day during which the particular species they are visiting secretes nectar, that they spend the remainder of the day in their nest. When the time approaches for nectar secretion to begin, the bees congregate near the nest entrance.

Bees collecting pollen sometimes deliberately 'scrabble' over the anthers to do so, while others become dusted with pollen incidentally, while they are primarily collecting nectar. In either circumstance, the bee's body – and especially its thorax – becomes covered with thousands and sometimes millions of pollen grains. The bee combs the pollen from its body and into its corbiculae. At the end of a foraging trip the pellets of pollen formed in the corbiculae, known collectively as a pollen load, weigh about 20 mg. About ten such pollen loads are necessary to provide sufficient pollen and fat to nourish one larva during its development; to keep its brood fed a colony needs to collect well over a million loads of pollen a year!

Most flower species make pollen available throughout the day, but

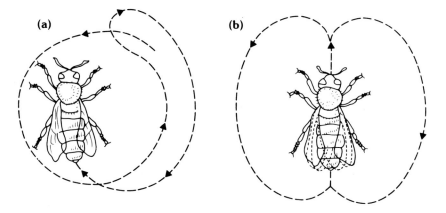

Figure 3.19 Honeybee dances: (a) the round dance and (b) the tail-wagging dance (after K. von Frisch).

usually there is a period when it is most abundant, and the time at which this occurs tends to be characteristic of the species concerned. For example, most field bean pollen is available in the afternoon when the flowers first open, and although nectar-gathering honeybees are most abundant in crops of field bean in the morning, the pollen gatherers tend to be restricted to the afternoon.

The regular rhythm of pollen collection is also subject to fluctuations in association with changing weather conditions, although probably less so than with nectar collection. Pollen collection is usually intensive after a period of unfavourable weather; this is partly because bees respond readily to an improvement in foraging conditions, but partly because the lack of pollen collection has generated an increased need for it inside the nests.

Communication of crops

> He ran and laughed behind a bee;
> And danced for very ecstasy!
>
> James Stephens, 'In the Poppy Field'

One of the most remarkable abilities of the honeybee is the communication by a successful forager of the location of favourable sources of nectar or pollen to the other members of its colony. This enables a colony rapidly to exploit a plentiful food supply and has undoubtedly been a major contribution in the success of the species.

When the source of forage is within about 25 m of the nest a successful forager on its return home may perform what is known as a 'round dance' on the comb surface. In this dance the forager makes a series of circles, and every one or two circles it alternates between a clockwise and an anticlockwise direction. Some of the bees nearby that are potential foragers appear to pay particular attention to the dance and 57

Figure 3.20 Forager (centre) performing a dance on return to its colony.

many attempt to follow it for part of its course. The dancing bee stops at intervals and regurgitates a drop of the nectar it has collected to the interested bees. Potential foragers learn the odour of the forage source from that of the nectar and from the odour adhering to the body of the dancing bee, and some of them eventually leave the nest to search for its location within a short radius of their colony.

This means of communication is remarkably effective, and in the right circumstances can result in a rapid increase in the number of foragers at a food source, the more numerous and lively the dances, the greater the increase in the number of recruits.

When the food source is distant from the hive its location by random searching would be tedious, if not ineffective, and the bees have overcome this by performing a dance that not only indicates the distance of the forage from the nest but also its direction.

In this dance, known as the 'waggle dance', the forager moves forward a short distance in a straight line or 'run', prescribes a semicircle back to the beginning of the run, moves to the top, and makes a semicircle back to the beginning of the run again, but this time in the reverse direction and on the opposite side. This process is repeated, often for several minutes. During the straight run, the bee rapidly waggles its abdomen. The duration of the straight run and the number of waggles increases with the distance of the food source from the nest.

The angle that the straight run differs from the vertical is the same as the angle between the food source, the nest entrance and the sun. While the successful forager is dancing it is closely observed and followed by

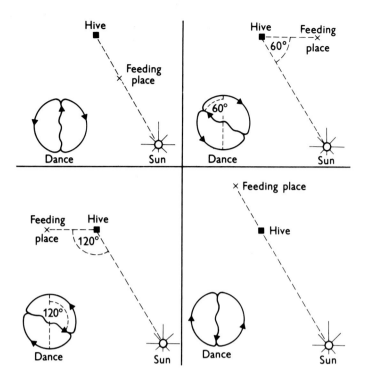

Figure 3.21 Relationship between the angle of the straight part of the tail wagging dance on the vertical comb, and the angle between the source of forage, sun and hive (after K. von Frisch).

other bees, who are able in some extraordinary way to transpose the set of information received from the dance to the situation in the field. How this is done is far from certain, but a remarkable proportion of the recruits that leave the nest arrive in the vicinity of the source of forage being communicated, although few probably go directly to the precise site indicated.

When it is remembered that a food source is likely to consist of several plants with a scattered distribution, and so would be exploited most efficiently if the arrival points of the recruits is likewise scattered, it is obviously desirable that the communication and interpretation of the location of a food source should not be too accurate.

Bees are sensitive to the plane of polarisation of light in the sky, so that on days when the sun is obscured they are able to deduce its position even when only a small area of clear sky is visible, and so they can orientate correctly in flight and make accurately orientated dances on their return home.

Without doubt, the directed recruits use the scent of the crop as a final aid to its location. However, not all sources of forage have an odour. This is especially true of sources of water. In such circumstances the foraging bees themselves compensate for the lack of floral scent by releasing their own Nasonov gland odour (pheromone) at the site, and so help by scent-marking the target area for recruits searching in the vicinity. It is interesting that however attractive a food source, bees do

59

not dance on their return home nor expose their Nasonov glands at the site until they have made a number of trips to it. This delay acts as a precautionary measure, and must have the biological advantage of not recruiting bees to a source that may be of a very transient nature.

Other pheromones produced by the bodies of bees probably help to attract recruits, or perhaps even to repel them from flowers that have just been visited. We still have much to learn about foraging behaviour.

Foraging method

> And, as it works, th' industrious bee
> Computes its time as well as we.
>
> Andrew Marvell, 'Thoughts in a Garden'

One of the characteristics of the honeybee that make it such a valuable pollinator is its readiness to visit many flower species and flowers of many different shapes and sizes. However, at any one time the bees of a colony collect most of their forage from only a few of the plant species available in the vicinity. This is undoubtedly a reflection of the honeybee's ability to communicate and exploit favourable sources of forage.

Furthermore, even colonies located side by side may utilise the local flora in different ways. This is partly because bees have an innate preference for certain species, and this preference varies from colony to colony, partly because a colony can acquire a 'taste' for certain pollens, and partly because of chance differences in the discoveries of bees that are searching for new crops.

One of the characteristics of the honeybee that has been well known since the time of Aristotle is the strong tendency for individuals to confine their attention to one flower species during a single foraging trip. Charles Darwin pointed out that this fidelity enables the bee to forage more quickly than if it had to discover afresh the sites of the nectaries on every flower it visited, and furthermore it enables the bee to keep to a flower species that is yielding abundant nectar or pollen. This flower constancy is, of course, most important in that it increases the chances that cross-pollination between flowers of the same species will occur.

The degree of constancy shown by an individual bee can be determined by examining microscopically the composition of its pollen pellets because each plant species produces distinctive pollen grains of characteristic shape and size. When the pollen pellet contains one type of pollen only, the bee has been constant throughout its trip. The proportion of different pollens present in a pollen pellet is influenced very much by the environment, and bees are usually more faithful when

60

there are large areas of attractive species than when there are many species and comparatively few plants of each.

Bees tend to remain faithful to a plant species on consecutive trips and days as long as it continues to yield sufficiently abundant and attractive nectar and pollen. On days when a particular species is temporarily not producing nectar or pollen, bees conditioned to collecting from it usually do not forage, and only a few change to another species. But when forage is still unavailable after more than a day or so this temporary fixation gives way to adaptability and the bees seek or become recruited to other crops. For example, in one series of observations it was found that only about half the foragers remained constant to the pollen which they were collecting a week previously.

Whenever possible bees prefer to forage near their nests; and so use less fuel and time in flying to and fro. However, the overriding factor that governs foraging distance is often the quality of the forage available.

Once a bee has found a favourable location in which to forage it does not range indiscriminately over it but tends to keep to a comparatively small area and to return to the vicinity in subsequent foraging trips. In general, the more prolific the food supply, the smaller the foraging area, but as the food supply becomes meagre the foraging areas expand until the visits are no longer economically viable and the area is abandoned altogether.

Even when the foraging area of a bee is small, it frequently moves from plant to plant. Usually only some of the flowers on a plant are open at any one time, but even so bees rarely forage on a plant until they have visited all the open flowers, or more than a small proportion of flowers on a flower head of a plant such as a sunflower or clover.

This behaviour must favour cross-pollination between flowers of the same species and is another way in which the behaviour of bees is well adapted to increase the seed production of the flowers they visit, and hence helps to ensure a continuing source of forage.

Seasonal cycle of colony growth

Such are the busy throng, whose numbers swell
The peopled hive, and frame the polish'd cell.

John Evans, 'The Bees'

In temperate climates the seasonal cycles determine the availability of flowers, and in other parts of the world forage may be severely curtailed during unfavourable seasons. In the absence of forage, as in many winter months, the colony has to survive on the pollen and honey it has

61

stored during times of plenty; the colony size diminishes and little if any brood is reared.

In these circumstances relatively few bees are engaged in brood rearing and most are idle. But idleness is fortunately associated with increased longevity and, with the appearance of flowers in the spring or the onset of other favourable circumstances, these workers are still available to forage; indeed the number of workers foraging increases until no more can be spared from brood rearing.

Increase in the amount of forage collected, and especially of pollen, stimulates greater brood production. Just how this is achieved is not known. Probably bees attending the queen increase her egg production by giving her more food, and probably more cells are prepared by the workers to receive the queen's eggs. Worker bees can also regulate the amount of brood to be reared by destroying some of the eggs or young larvae, but the factors that decide whether they do so and which ones are selected are largely unknown. Rearing of more brood creates a greater demand for food that in turn appears to increase the tempo of all colony activities, and in particular stimulates more foraging. Probably the increased amount of brood results in the nest bees preparing more cells to receive pollen, so the pollen gatherers take less time to find cells to deposit their loads. Similarly, the increased demand for nectar probably encourages house bees to accept loads of nectar from foragers more quickly at the hive entrance, and so both the nectar gatherers and the pollen gatherers spend less time in the nest and more in the field.

As long as forage continues to be readily available the increased brood rearing that follows increased foraging will enlarge the adult population, and so the number of bees able to care for brood or to forage also increases. The increased activity of the individual bees at this stage of intensive colony growth results in their length of life diminishing to its lowest level for the year, and bees that emerge in May or June may live only for 4–5 weeks.

Colony growth eventually enables the queen to attain her maximum rate of egg laying; when this is achieved the proportion of adult bees to brood increases so that proportionally more bees are available to forage. At this stage of its development the colony reaches its peak ability to build up surplus stores of nectar and pollen to tide it over dearth periods, or to make surplus honey for the beekeeper.

Co-ordination of activities

For among Bees and Ants are social systems found
so complex and well-ordered as to invite offhand
a pleasant fable enough: that once upon a time,

or ever a man was born to rob their honeypots,
bees were fully endow'd with Reason and only lost it
by ordering so their life as to dispense with it;
whereby it pined away and perish'd of disuse.
                    Robert Bridges, 'The Testament of Beauty'

We have seen how the frequency of transfer of food from bee to bee enables knowledge of the quality and quantity of food being collected, and of a colony's food requirements, to rapidly spread among the inhabitants. Apart from being a form of communication itself, the food that is transferred may also contain chemical 'messages' (pheromones), which can either cause physiological changes in the bee that receives them or cause it to modify its behaviour. Thus food transfer helps to bind the honeybee colony together as a coherent whole.

During recent years research workers have come to realise the importance of many different types of pheromone in controlling the activities of the honeybee colony. In the darkness of the hive or nest vision is of no importance, and there is little communication by sound, but communication by chemical means is of great significance.

We have seen that in bumblebee colonies the inhibition of the reproductive tendencies of the workers may be largely psychological, and a queen bumblebee diminishes the likelihood of her workers laying eggs by actively dominating them, the workers being able to recognise the queen by her characteristic scent.

In contrast, the queen honeybee uses a more sophisticated method.

Figure 3.22 Worker bees palpating their queen's abdomen with their antennae. One is also licking it.

She produces a pheromone from 'mandibular' glands inside her head, which becomes distributed over her body. Whenever the queen stops moving on a comb she is surrounded by a 'court' of nearby workers, which face towards her, offer her food, lick her and touch her with their antennae.

Recent research has indicated that as a result of palpating the queen with their antennae, the workers in a queen's court obtain pheromone on them. In a honeybee colony workers frequently make antennal contact with each other without food transfer taking place. It seems that during this contact queen pheromone may be transferred from bee to bee. Workers that have been in a queen's court and palpated her with their antennae have an increased tendency to make antennal contact with other workers. But it is the other workers that mainly initiate the contact, suggesting they can detect the presence of the queen pheromone on the antennae of workers from the court. The queen pheromone that these workers receive is then distributed to other bees in the colony so all are aware of the presence of their queen.

The recipients of this pheromone are inhibited from rearing new queens. Perhaps this pheromone has evolved from the distinctive scent produced by the queen or other dominant individuals present in communities of less advanced social bees.

Queen production

> But when two twin-born monarchs burst to day,
> Claiming with equal rights a sovereign's sway.
>
> John Evans, 'The Bees'

When the queen of a colony dies or becomes old, the supply of her pheromones is curtailed or diminished, with the result that her workers are no longer completely inhibited and new queens are produced. These queens are reared in special large cells that hang downward, and are eventually about 25 mm long and taper towards the tip. Queens, like workers, are produced from fertilised eggs, but, as we have seen, the larvae that hatch from them are fed entirely on a glandular secretion produced by the workers. This 'royal jelly' is much in demand as a human health food, and many beekeepers manage their colonies in special ways to produce it for sale. It appears that a special differentiating factor is also added to the diet of queen larvae which helps to determine that they grow into queens, but much needs to be discovered about this.

Queen rearing is especially likely to occur as the colony is expanding and the available pheromone is diluted among the worker population.

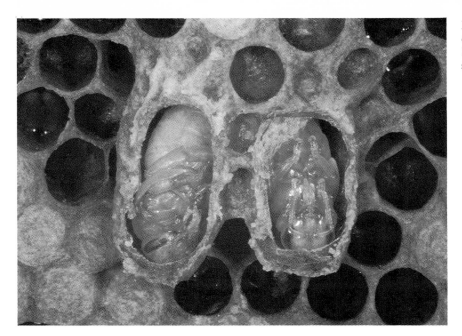

Figure 3.23 Two queen cells whose sides have been removed to show the pupae inside.

Usually, up to about ten young developing queens may be reared, rarely more. Workers that visit queen cells appear to obtain pheromone from the queens which they distribute by antennal contact with other workers and in transferred food.

The first of the queens to emerge attempts to kill the others while they are still helpless in their cells, but often she fails to find or dispose of all of them, and more than one young queen becomes free on the combs. When two young queens meet each immediately recognises a rival and they engage in mortal combat.

The sole survivor will mate within a few days of her emergence and soon afterwards will begin to lay eggs. Her pheromone production is greater than that of the old queen and sufficient to inhibit the workers from rearing additional queens. If the old queen has survived she is sometimes killed at this stage by the young queen who has superseded her but sometimes both may live and lay eggs in the colony for some weeks before the old queen succumbs.

Mating

> Dream of a duel they will win inevitably,
> A curtain of wax dividing them from the bride flight,
> The upflight of the murderess into a heaven that loves her.
> Sylvia Plath, 'The Bee Meeting'

True honeybees Because mating occurs many metres above ground level, we know too little about it. Apparently, a flying drone is able to detect the odour of a queen when about 50 m away and flies towards its source. As a result, in favourable conditions a 'comet' of hundreds of males may be seen chasing after a single queen. During fine weather, drone honeybees often congregate and fly continuously in restricted areas, about 100 m in diameter, and about 30 m above the ground. Such drone congregation areas are likely to occur in hilly or mountainous areas, but not in flat country without prominent landmarks. Congregation areas are sometimes used for several years in succession. Apparently, queens are attracted to these areas and so the chance of drones finding a mate must be considerably enhanced.

When about a metre from the queen the drone can probably see her, but before he actually attempts to copulate he needs to examine her with his legs and antennae. If he is satisfied, copulation is violent and soon completed. The drone's genitalia are explosively everted into the sting chamber of the queen; he is unable to withdraw them and they are left behind when he literally 'tears' himself away. Soon afterwards he dies. Thus only unsuccessful drones manage to return home! Inside the nest, drones show no interest in a queen, whether she be a virgin or mated. So, in common with most behaviour patterns, mating of the honeybee only occurs in certain environmental circumstances. The males respond to only a few of the many possible features of a queen; in fact a drone will readily 'mate' with a crude wooden model of a queen provided it is coated with the correct queen odour, and has a hole bored into it of similar size and depth to that of the queen's sting chamber.

Although the drone dies after a single mating, the queen may mate with up to ten drones in quick succession; if her sperm storage sac, or spermatheca, still contains insufficient sperm, she may make another flight in a day or so.

Drones are normally evicted from a colony when forage becomes scarce at the end of the season, but if the colony does not possess a mated queen no eviction occurs. This helps to ensure a supply of drones to mate with any virgin queens that are eventually produced. However, as soon as a virgin queen has mated and begun to lay eggs, drones are of no further value to the colony, so their lives are forfeited.

Swarming

> The task is easy: but to clip the wings
> Of their high-flying arbitrary kings:
> At their command, the people swarm away:
> Confine the tyrant, and the slaves will stay.
>
> Virgil, *Georgics*

66

A colony also produces young queens when it reproduces by swarming. *Swarming*
It appears that swarming, like the process of queen supersedure, is
initiated by a deficit of queen pheromone, but swarming is more likely to
occur in late spring and early summer, when the swarm will have several
weeks to become established and accumulate sufficient food for the
winter.

A swarm itself consists of the old queen, and a proportion, usually
about half, of the worker and drone population. Because a laying queen
is too heavy to fly, the bees cease to feed their queen several days before
swarming is imminent, so she ceases to lay and her abdomen shrinks.
The swarm usually leaves its parent colony a day or so before the young
queen emerges, amidst much excitement and many bees buzzing and
running over the comb surface. The bees of the swarm fly off as a well
defined group, but soon come to rest and cluster together on a tree
branch, fence post or other support that acts as a temporary home for
anything from an hour to some days. Often this temporary home is
within a short distance of their old nest, but as long as the queen remains
within the swarm none of the bees will forsake it and return home.

The cluster consists of an outer shell about three bees thick, and
a loosely packed interior. After the swarm has been settled for an hour
or so, an entrance hole to the interior can be clearly seen.

Bees of a clustered swarm are usually tranquil and in an ideal state for
a beekeeper to collect and establish in one of his hives. However,
whereas most bees are quiescent, a few search actively for a permanent
nest site for the future colony. When a scout bee has discovered a likely
nest site, on its return it performs a dance on the side of the swarm

Figure 3.24
A honeybee swarm.

cluster in which it indicates the direction and distance of the site, in the same way that a successful forager indicates the location of a food source. The scout bee returns to the potential nest site at intervals and 'marks' it with the odour from its Nasonov gland. Other bees that are stimulated to visit the site may also dance on their return.

When two or more sites have been discovered the dances taking place on the cluster surface may indicate different locations, but usually the majority of the scouts become converted to one or other of the sites. When two sites discovered are of equal attractiveness the one furthest away tends to be selected; this obviously has the biological advantage of diminishing competition between the swarm and its parent colony.

The departure of the swarm from its temporary to its permanent home is once again preceded by many bees running over the comb surface and buzzing with their wings. Once airborne the swarm is guided to the nest site by scout bees and is maintained as a coherent whole by the release of Nasonov pheromone and queen pheromone. Entrance into the new nest site is accompanied by much fanning and Nasonov gland exposure. It is now possible to attract swarms to empty hives using synthetic Nasonov pheromone.

Before the bees of a swarm leave their maternal colony they fill their honey-stomachs from stores in the comb, and, because clustered bees are relatively inactive, they still carry ample food reserves with them to the new nest site, where it provides a ready source of raw material for comb construction.

No sooner is the nest-site occupied than some bees begin to secrete wax and build comb and others start to forage. The queen rapidly gains in weight again, and as soon as the first cells are built she is ready to lay eggs in them.

Once brood has been reared in a cell it is favoured for storing nectar or pollen, so as a colony grows there is a tendency for the comb that was built first to be used for storing food, and for brood rearing to be pushed to the more recently built comb in the centre of the nest.

Soon after the old queen and swarm have left the mother colony, one of the new queens that have been reared will emerge, and, provided the colony does not swarm again, she disposes of her rivals as when a colony is superseding its old queen. Sometimes, however, depending on colony size and other factors, the colony may produce another swarm, and if this happens the first queen to emerge will go with it and the next to emerge will eventually head the mother colony. In these circumstances the first queen to emerge will produce a characteristic 'piping' sound and the queens still in their cells produce a characteristic 'quacking' sound. It is likely that these sounds cause the workers to keep all but the one virgin confined in their cells and so prevent mortal combat until the swarm has departed.

The relatively small adult populations of both the mother colony and
swarm ensure that the individual bees receive adequate pheromone to
inhibit further queen rearing.

Control of nest environment

The white hive is snug as a virgin,
Sealing off her brood cells, her honey, and quietly humming.
Sylvia Plath, 'The Bee Meeting'

Pheromones produced by the queen not only inhibit queen rearing but
have the opposite effect of stimulating other activities including comb
building, brood rearing, foraging and food storage. Because in small
colonies the individual bees receive a greater amount of pheromone
than the bees in large colonies, they are also stimulated to greater
activity. This is, of course, of great importance in ensuring the rapid
growth and development of swarms and small colonies, so that they
have sufficient bees and sufficient food stores to survive unfavourable
seasons.

Much of the successful distribution of the honeybee in the world is
dependent on the ability of the colony to control the environment
independently of outside conditions, and to survive on food stored in its
combs during winter or other unfavourable seasons when it cannot
forage.

A colony has two methods of combating cold. First, the bees act to
reduce heat loss by clustering together. As the temperature falls the
cluster becomes more compact so decreasing its surface and heat loss.
A compact cluster may contain as many as 21 bees per cubic inch (1.3
bees per cubic centimetre). Secondly, a colony can react to increased
cold by eating and metabolising more food and so generating more heat.
By a combination of these methods a colony can survive temperatures as
low as $-40\,°C$.

Equally spectacular is a colony's ability to survive high temperatures.
As the temperature rises the bees tend to move further apart on the
combs until some leave the nest altogether and cluster outside. With
further increase some bees near the entrance begin to fan with their
wings and so create a current of air through the nest.

Finally, bees make use of the evaporation of water or dilute nectar to
cool their colony. They spread minute droplets in the cells and leave
them to evaporate, and also aid evaporation themselves by drawing out
thin films of water with their mouthparts.

As a result of these regulatory activities the temperatures in the part
of the colony where brood is being reared are maintained at about
$35\,°C$ even when temperatures outside the nest are as high as $70\,°C$.

　　Thus the individuals of a honeybee colony, by acting together, are able successfully to survive conditions in which the individual would most certainly succumb, and so the colony can flourish and reproduce when favourable conditions return.

Although we can marvel at the organisation and behaviour of the honeybee society, we are still far from understanding the mechanism by which it is organised, and especially how the activities of thousands of individuals, each with its own behavioural repertoire, are co-ordinated to function as a coherent whole.

4 *Stingless honeybees*

> How skilfully she builds her cell!
> How neat she spreads the wax;
> And labours hard to store it well
> With the sweet food she makes.
>
> Isaac Watts, 'Against Idleness and Mischief'

Evolution

The stingless honeybees (Meliponini), like the true honeybees *(Apis)*, have attained the very peak of social organisation. It is supposed that these tropical stingless bees were the first to develop social behaviour, and did so before the true honeybees and bumblebees had evolved from their common social or semi-social ancestor.

The stingless honeybees occur in the Tropics and sub-Tropics of South America, the southern half of Africa and southeastern Asia. They comprise many genera and species, but there are two main genera, the *Trigona* and the *Melipona*, the latter being the larger bees. Colonies of the *Melipona* comprise 500–4000 adults and those of *Trigona* from 300 to 80 000. The bees of different species exhibit a large variation in size and appearance; some are slender, others burly, some hairy, and others nearly hairless and shiny.

There is much to learn about the life cycle and behaviour of the various species, but it is already clear that their early evolutionary divergence has resulted in some marked and important differences between their behaviour and that of the true honeybee, especially those differences concerned with nest architecture, food storage, larval feeding and means of crop communication.

Defence

> And when their sovereign's quarrel calls them out,
> His foes to mortal combat they defy,
> And think it honour at his feet to die.
>
> Virgil, *Georgics*

Stingless bees are named from the fact that although they possess stings these are vestigial and cannot be used in defence. However, most species are able to defend their colonies very efficiently. Some bite their

71

enemy or burn his skin with a caustic fluid. Others swarm all over their victim, and especially into his nose, ears and eyes, and generally demoralise him. Sometimes a stingless bee locks its mandibles so tightly on its victim that its head tears loose from its body before its grip can be broken. So complete is their defence that many species of stingless bee are almost immune from attack by other insects.

Nest structure

> And many a thought did I build up on thought,
> As the wild bee hangs cell to cell.
>
> Robert Browning, 'Pauline'

Most species of meliponines nest in hollow trees, although a few occupy the deserted nests of termites and ants, often at some depth under the ground. The nest is constructed of a mixture of wax and resin or propolis from plants. Basically it consists of a group of brood cells, often surrounded by a soft sheath, the 'involucrum', adjacent to which are large cells, resembling those of bumblebees, in which honey and pollen are stored. However, unlike the storage cells of bumblebees and honeybees, they are never first used for brood rearing.

Sometimes the honey and pollen are stored in separate pots. The more primitive of the *Trigona* have simple nests, resembling those of bumblebees, in which are spherical pots to hold the honey and tall waxen tubes for storing pollen. Sometimes the honey and pollen are intermixed in the same pot.

The brood and storage area of a meliponine colony is supported by a

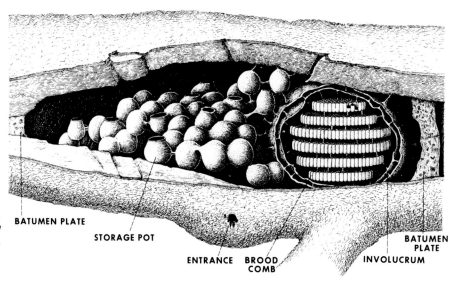

Figure 4.1
A meliponine colony
(from C. D. Michener,
after J. M. F.
de Camargo).

BATUMEN PLATE

STORAGE POT

ENTRANCE BROOD
COMB

BATUMEN
PLATE

INVOLUCRUM

Figure 4.2
A meliponine colony
established in a rustic
hive. The involucrum
enclosing brood cells is
on the left and large
storage cells are on the
right.

series of pillars and the whole is enclosed in a hard outer layer, the 'batumen'. The outer layer of exposed nests also incorporates chewed plant material. When nests occur in hollow trees or other large cavities, the batumen seals off an area suitable in size for the nest.

The nest entrance often projects as an external tube; sometimes it is also continued internally along the wall of the cavity, which has the effect of 'directing' successful foragers to the food storage area of the nest.

The brood cells are vertical and the cell opening is at the top. Commonly they are arranged in a series of horizontal combs. In contrast to honeybees and bumblebees, but like many solitary bees, the brood cells of the meliponines are mass provisioned. These provisions consist of glandular secretions produced by the workers mixed with honey and pollen. The queen lays her egg on this semi-fluid mixture, and then the cell is sealed with a cap.

In one species at least, a worker lays an egg in the cell just before the queen is ready to do so. The queen eats the worker egg, presumably benefiting from the nourishment it provides, and probably eats some of the larval food before laying an egg of her own. When the larvae are fully grown and have spun their cocoons, the workers remove the wax, exposing the cocoons, as happens in bumblebee colonies, leaving sufficient wax between the cocoons to bind them together.

New cells are constructed at the margins of the comb until they extend to the wall of the nest cavity. The workers either start to build new combs above the centre of the preceding one, or by an upward spiral 73

Figure 4.3 Part of a meliponine colony. The 'involucrum' over the brood cells and the covering of a storage cell (top right) has been removed.

continuation of it. By the time that the top of the brood cavity has been filled with cells, adult bees will be emerging from the lowest comb; when emergence is complete the empty cocoons are removed and cell building begins again.

Reproduction

> While the keen scouts with curious eye explore
>   The rifted roof, or widely gaping floor
> Of some time-shatter'd pile, or hollow'd oak
>   Proud in decay, or cavern of the rock.
>
> John Evans, 'The Bees'

The swarming behaviour of the meliponines contrasts with that of the true honeybee, *Apis mellifera*. When a new site for the swarm has been discovered, workers of the swarm take with them, from the parental nest, materials with which to build the new one. In fact, they make many visits back to the parental nest to collect building materials and food. They carry pollen and honey from the old nest in a liquid suspension in their honey-stomachs. In their new home they first seal any cracks in the nest cavity, and then construct the involucrum, pillars, storage pots and brood cells.

Only when the first brood cells have been constructed and all else is ready does a queen from the old colony join the workers of the swarm, or, more correctly, is escorted to the new site by a group of bees. In further contrast to the *Apis* honeybees, it is a new queen and not the old one that joins the swarm.

74

Migration of a young queen, instead of an old one, has the obvious biological advantage that continuity of brood rearing in the mother colony is maintained, and the mother queen does not need to lose weight and so cease egg production before taking flight. This alone may help to explain why the mother colony can afford to provide so generously for the swarm.

Soon after the arrival of the young queen at the new nest she leaves again to mate. Aggregations of hundreds or thousands of males are often present in the air near to the new nest, so ensuring that mating soon occurs; such large numbers of males must also help to minimise the likelihood that the queen is seized by a predator. However, unlike the honeybee, she mates once only. She returns home with the genitalia of the successful male still inserted in her.

Communication of forage

> While honey lies in Every Flower, no doubt,
> It takes a Bee to get the Honey out.
> Arthur Guthernon, 'A Poet's Proverbs'

The meliponines are also most interesting in that various species exhibit differing abilities in communicating sources of forage; some systems are akin to the possible excitement that a returned bumblebee forager may engender among its nest mates, while others approach the sophisticated communication in a honeybee colony.

Probably one of the simplest forms of communication occurs in the nest of some *Trigona* species in which the inmates of a colony use the odour of the flowers on a returned forager's body to discover the source of forage, and no information on the direction or distance of the forage is provided. In other species the returned foragers make a zig-zag 'buzzing' run, reminiscent of that made by *Apis* honeybees on a swarm cluster. Jostling by such bees undoubtedly serves to bring about a general increase in activity within the nest, and so perhaps encourages other bees to leave to forage. At a slightly more advanced stage of communication, some of the inmates of the nest repeat the characteristic sounds made by the returned forager, and it soon spreads through the colony, inducing a large exodus of would-be foragers.

Other species of *Trigona* assist recruits to find the source of food by marking it with a pheromone from their mandibular glands, which appears to be analogous to marking of food sources with Nasonov gland pheromone by the true honeybee. Foragers of yet another species go a stage further and mark an odour trail from nest to food source; when a forager has satisfied itself that the food source is worthy of new recruits,

Stingless honeybees it alights at short intervals of a few metres or so on its way home and secretes a series of odoriferous marks on vegetation or on the ground. Odour trails can be particularly effective when the food source is well above ground level, such as in the tree-tops; the honeybee *Apis mellifera* lacks the ability to communicate such a site.

Unlike the *Trigona*, bees of the species *Melipona* do not use odour trails, but it appears that successful *Melipona* foragers 'guide' potential recruits for a short distance to the food source and also use a system of communication in which the returned foragers produce a series of bursts of sound, the durations of which appear to increase with the distance to the food source. Use of sound language is also thought to occur in the dance language of the true honeybee, but proof that these sounds influence the bees that perceive them, and that they alone are sufficient to direct recruits to the forage concerned, seems to be lacking. There is much to be discovered.

Part III

Beekeeping: past and present

5 How beekeeping began

The bee is more honoured than other animals, not because she labours, but because she labours for others.

St John Chrysostom, *Homilies*

For many thousands of years before man was a beekeeper, he was a honey hunter, and robbed natural nests of honeybees of their accumulated stores of food. Indeed honey was the only form of sweetening material that was available to him. But for many primitive people honey seems to have been even more important for its strong magico-religious significance, and has often been used as a medicine rather than a food.

The transition from honey hunting to beekeeping, that is from collecting honey from wild colonies in caves and hollow trees to keeping honeybee colonies in hives, was a slow but natural process. It probably occurred many times in different parts of the world, and the entire sequence of stages can still be discovered today in various regions.

However, it must be pointed out at the onset that even in the most modern of bee farms, the bee used is still not a truly domesticated animal. Up to the present time the beekeeper has changed the behaviour of his bees very little, if at all. Man has made some progress in breeding bees with what he considers to be desirable characteristics, such as a diminished tendency to swarm or to attack, but for the most part man merely exploits the behaviour patterns and the tendencies that are already present.

Honey hunting in prehistoric times

The oak is on their hills; the topmost tree
Bears the rich acorn, and the trunk the bee.

Hesiod, *Ancient Greece*

Honey is a desirable prize for many animals and before we discuss the surviving evidence of primitive man's interest in honey it is interesting to realise that other primates are also honey hunters and like man they may use 'tools' to accomplish their purpose. Both of our two examples are from Tanzania.

In 1957, F. G. Merfield and H. Millar described coming across eight chimpanzees gathered round the entrance to an underground nest, probably of a meliponine bee:

Each . . . held a long twig which it poked down the hole and withdrew coated with honey. There was only one hole, and though for the most part they took turns at using their twigs, quarrels were constantly breaking out, and those who had licked off most of their honey tried to snatch the newly-coated twigs. . . . This is one of the few examples I have known of a wild animal employing a tool.

Similar behaviour was recorded by K. Izawa and J. Itani in 1966. They observed a female chimpanzee, whose mouth was smeared with yellow honey, using a small twig to get honey from a *Trigona* nest in a hollow tree. They, also, were impressed by this fine example of tool-using behaviour and thought that if the chimpanzee had not used the twig she probably would have been unable to get at the honey.

The use of tools by honey-gathering primates leads us naturally to primitive man. For evidence of his honey-hunting activities we are fortunate to have a rich heritage of cave paintings; some from Altamira in northern Spain indicate that honey hunting occurred as long ago as the end of the Ice Age.

However, the most renowned evidence of honey hunting in prehistoric times comes from a Mesolithic, or Middle Stone Age, painting (about 7000 BC) in a rock shelter near Valencia, in eastern Spain. It depicts a figure, who has climbed a rope, probably of woven sedge grass, to a nest of honeybees in a small cavity on a cliff face. He is surrounded by angry bees while transferring honeycomb to a basket he carries with him. The beekeeper must indeed have valued his prize, especially as he appears to be wearing little or no protective clothing. Perhaps then, as is so often the case now, the honey had a mystic significance.

The reason why prehistoric man painted or drew on the walls of caves is of course pure conjecture, but it is currently often supposed that the paintings were thought to help in some way towards the successful outcome of a future hunting expedition. Perhaps this painting was made to help the bee hunters find the bees' nests, and not to succumb under pressure from too many stings!

Lya Dams has recently discovered other Mesolithic rock paintings depicting bees and honey gathering in the same area of eastern Spain. The bees are represented by small crosses, dots or shaped blobs in various shades of reddish brown. Sometimes they are isolated groups inside small rock crevices or on rock protuberances. When human or animal figures also occur the bees are of a similar size. One superb rock painting illustrates five men on a ladder reaching to a bees' nest; several bees are nearly as large as the men and look as if they are about to attack. At the base of the ladder a group of men and women are watching and perhaps waiting for the spoils.

These paintings are not isolated examples. A series of no fewer than 80 primitive rock paintings done by bushmen in southern Africa, all of

Figure 5.1 Recently discovered painting of a honey gathering expedition in a rock shelter of the Cingle de la Eremita del Barranc Fondo, Valltorta Gorge, Castellon, Spain.

which depict various aspects of beekeeping, have been discovered. Recent research has indicated that bees, along with the eland and various mythical creatures, probably played an important part in magico-religious purposes and practices, and often bees and other motifs occur together. In one rock shelter, in the Royal Natal National Park, a swarm of bees can be seen accompanying a mythical elephant-man. As it does not appear that any of the bees were in fact stinging him, perhaps this emphasises primitive man's belief that their gods, like themselves, were fond of honey.

81

Figure 5.2 Rock painting of mythical elephant-man with accompanying swarm of bees in Royal Natal National Park.

Several other rock paintings in southern Africa depict honeybee swarms, honeycombs, bees' nests and bee hunters at work. The bee hunters are using various types of ladder to reach the nest; one of the ladders branches into two at the top, probably to make room for two bee hunters working side by side.

A rock painting near the Toghwana Dam in the Matopo Hills of Zimbabwe is particularly interesting because it shows a honey hunter who is smoking the colony. Blowing smoke at bees causes them to gorge themselves with honey from the combs, and so they carry some of their colony's food reserves with them if forced, by fire, to vacate their nest. Once they have filled their honey-stomachs they are less inclined to sting. Before examining a colony today, beekeepers still puff smoke at it to subdue the bees. Although the modern beekeeper now uses a special 'smoker' consisting of a fire pot and bellows, it is sobering to realise that the subduing effect of smoke had already been discovered by primitive man. It is likely that this practice arose independently in many parts of the world and is a logical outcome of the primitive use of fire to ward off wild beasts.

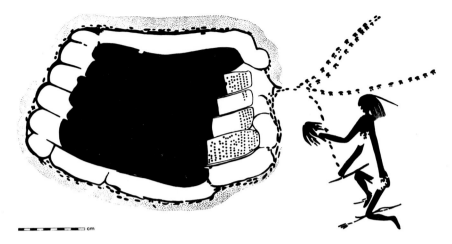

It has been suggested that the combs in the Toghwana Dam rock painting are depicted as if seen from below, and that the dark areas represent comb filled with honey or capped brood, and the light areas represent empty comb. The dots could represent cells filled with larvae or pollen – more likely the latter, as pollen is often deposited near to the entrance where these cells occur.

Honey hunting today

I went to the forest to collect honey.
I went, I went, I went.
I went very far, beyond the big river.
I heard the sound of bees. I saw up high the place of honey.
I said, 'Nobody has enclosed the tree with vine, it is mine; it is my honey'.
I sharpened my axe, very sharp indeed.
I cut a vine. I fanned my fire, and put the fire in my basket.
I began to climb; I climbed, I climbed.
The honey was very far. It was honey, real honey, not apuma.
I reached it. I fastened the vine, I sat. I put fire into the hole.
I blew. I got much smoke, I drove out many bees.
I chopped, I chopped, I chopped.

Song of African Mbuti Pygmies

Honey is still prized among primitive societies today as their only form of sweetening, as it was of course for primitive man, and often they eat the comb, wax, honey, pollen and brood in its entirety. It is often assumed, and probably for the most part rightly so, that the practices of primitive people today reflect those of ancient man. Many of the honey-gathering methods employed by ancient man, including the use of ropes, bags, baskets, chopping axe and knife, have probably survived almost unchanged among many peoples today, including the Zulus,

83

Hottentots, Massai and Pygmies of Africa where honey hunting is still
widespread. Honey is and was valued as an energy-producing food
among the hunters and nomads; when on expeditions the Massai
warrior would survive for days on honey alone.

Colin Turnbull has provided us with the following interesting account
of honey gathering by the Epulu pygmies of the Congo:

> Of all the many foods in the forest, honey calls the pygmies more strongly
> than any. At all times of the year there is game to be caught, different kinds
> of mushrooms and fruits and nuts and berries to be gathered, but the forest
> only gives its people honey during two happy months. It gives with even
> greater abundance, however, and the honey season is a season for aban-
> doned merrymaking, where even the cares of hunting become unimportant
> as each individual, young or old, man or woman, sets off every morning in
> the quest of this precious gift. Above all, it is a season for rejoicing, for
> dancing and singing.
>
> Almost every hour someone returned from a secret forage, with leaf
> bundles tied to his belt, dripping the sticky liquid down his legs. Sometimes it
> was too liquified to be eaten, and then the whole bundle was simply dipped
> into a bowl of clear forest water, making a sweet tasting drink. But far more
> popular was the whole comb which could be eaten, grubs, larvae, bees and
> all. If it was very hard then it was softened over the fire first, and this made
> the grubs squirm more actively so that the honey worked its way down your
> throat.

Turnbull further relates that so great was the desire for honey by one
pygmy that although his wedding was imminent, he hastened off to
collect some honey he had just heard about although it was several days
journey through the forest. However, evidently the honey he obtained
had a pacifying effect on him, because after marrying on his return he
was able to report to his in-laws that his wife was satisfactory and that it
had not been necessary to beat her at all often!

Throughout much of Asia, honey hunting still contributes more to the
total honey crop produced than from bees kept in hives, however primitive. It is not of course confined to *Apis mellifera* and *Apis cerana*. Even
if the crop from an *Apis florea* is usually small, it can usually be stolen
without undue discomfort because the bees are not easily aroused. In
India, most of the crop comes from colonies of *Apis dorsata*, which can
be very fierce and build their combs high above the ground in trees or
rock overhangs. In Tibet, long bamboo ladders are suspended from the
tops of cliffs to reach *Apis dorsata* colonies sheltering under projecting
rocks on the cliff face. In the mountains of the southern part of the
Sultanate of Oman, ropes are used in a similar way to collect *Apis
mellifera* colonies.

Apis mellifera was not introduced into the Americas until the 17th
century, but stingless bees are indigenous to South and Central America

and there was already present a long established tradition of bee hunting
and beekeeping when the Spaniards invaded in the 16th century. Today,
honey from stingless bees still forms an important part of the diet of
some South American Indian tribes. They can easily collect nests that
are totally or partially exposed, but where nests are completely enclosed
the tribesmen are often forced to fell trees to obtain the honey, which is
sometimes enough to fill a hollow gourd.

Stingless bees do not restrict foraging to nectar and pollen but also
collect liquid from fruit and resins, and sometimes unsavoury sources
such as dead animals and excrement. Nevertheless, the honey produced
is highly favoured and thought to possess healing properties.

The honey obtained from many colonies of stingless bees is probably
present in small amounts only, probably no more than from a large
bumblebee colony. But even the little honey that can be harvested from
bumblebee colonies was, in the past, probably a welcome and tasty
addition to the diet of country folk throughout Europe.

F. W. L. Sladen, the great authority on bumblebees who lived early in
this century, reported that

> Under favourable conditions humble-bees store honey, the flavour of which,
> as most schoolboys know, is excellent; but, unfortunately, the amount in
> each nest never exceeds a few ounces, so that to obtain a quantity many
> colonies would have to be kept, and even then the work of collecting it would
> be laborious.

Gilbert White in his *Natural history of Selbourne* has immortalised a
village boy of the mid-18th century who made a practice of capturing
bumblebees and sucking the nectar from their honey-stomachs. There
was of course an earlier precedent for this behaviour; who does not
remember in William Shakespeare's *A midsummer night's dream* that
Bottom requested Cobweb to 'kill me a red hipt humble-bee on the top
of a thistle; and good monsieur, bring me the honey-bag'.

Honey hunters today, as presumably did those of long ago, employ
various aids to locate bees' nests. These include the shimmering of bees'
wings against the setting sun, the presence of bee faeces on the ground
in the vicinity of nests, and help from the honey guide bird *Indicator
indicator*. Many records, including those of Livingstone in 1855, refer to
the use of these birds. To retain the good services of a bird the hunter
must leave some honeycomb on the ground for it; there is a belief that if
this practice is not followed, then on the next occasion the bird will
deceive the hunter and lead him to a wild beast instead of a bees' nest.

Correct preparation for a honey-hunting expedition is frequently
regarded as of paramount importance to its success – probably a
reflection of the great mystical and magical powers conferred on honey,
and belief in the purity of the bees. Special emphasis is placed on the 85

need for chastity of those who gather honey. Some branches of the Nagus tribe, who inhabit hills between Assam and Burma, believe that from the day on which a honey-hunting expedition is arranged the participants must abstain from sexual intercourse; other, less strict branches of the tribe limit abstention to the night before setting off.

The Hadzapi, a hunting tribe in northern Tanzania, have learned to take only part of the comb from wild colonies and to leave the remainder to collect later in the year; undoubtedly the development of such a habit must have been one of the first steps from mere honey hunting to beekeeping as such, as it allowed the colony to live and provide additional harvests. But there would be little point in the finder not taking all the comb and food from a nest if somebody else who found it later did so. This inevitably led to wild colonies being owned, either by a group or by a single person, and this ownership must have been denoted in some way.

Honey hunting was not confined to the Tropics, and, in the Middle Ages, it was common in the woods and forests of northern Europe. Once the owner of a 'bee tree' had cut his own individual mark on the tree-trunk, his right to the honey was jealously guarded and defended by law. However, as is to be expected, there were frequent disputes over the ownership of these bee trees, whether occupied or not, and along with other possessions the bee trees were frequently mentioned in wills and other deeds.

The practice of claiming and marking nest-sites still occurs in the world today. In central Oman, the finder of a cave with an *Apis florea* colony builds a small pyramid of stones at the entrance to denote ownership. Returning to the Epulu pygmies of the Congo, we find that each small honey-hunting group claims 'certain honey trees for its own by marking them with a vine tied around the base, or some other sign that they know will be respected by all other pygmies'. The Kikuyu honey hunters of Kenya mark the trunk of a bee tree with the clan's as well as the owner's symbol, the implication being that any would-be thief will have the whole clan to contend with! The bushmen of South Africa had no personal possessions except bee colonies, and these were even inherited from one generation to another.

Transition from honey hunting to beekeeping

I will arise and go now, and go to Innisfree,
And a small cabin build there, of clay and wattles made:
Nine bean-rows will I have there, a hive for the honey-bee,
And live alone in the bee-loud glade.
William Butler Yeats, 'The Lake Isle of Innisfree'

We have seen that by using a little care the honey hunter would find that he could avoid killing the colony when he robbed it of honey, and that he could then gather another honey crop from it the following year, or even later the same season. From this stage of possessiveness it is easy to envisage a honey hunter claiming the rights to a honeybee colony that had established itself in a hollow log, and moving the log with its occupants near to his home so he could more easily guard it from robbers. Then he might collect some empty logs and put them in sites where he hoped bees would occupy them, or he might transfer combs and bees taken from trees to them, thus forming a small 'apiary' over which he or his family could keep constant vigilance.

Various stages of this evolutionary process can be seen in many parts of the world today. Many African communities still put artificial 'hives' of hollowed-out tree-trunks, cylinders of bark joined with wooden needles, basketry or pots in trees near wild colonies. These trap hives are either lodged into the branches of the trees or are suspended from the branches by ropes, baobab trees often being preferred. When trees are rare, the trap hives are often built into the walls of houses, or suspended under the eaves.

Attempts are made to increase the attractiveness of empty hives to swarms by many different methods. Hives are often smeared with honey or aromatic herbs; they are sometimes fumigated with smoke from burning wood; ripe bananas may be placed at the entrance; or they may even be coated with cow dung. Naturally enough occupation of these trap hives depends very much on chance and, as one would expect in

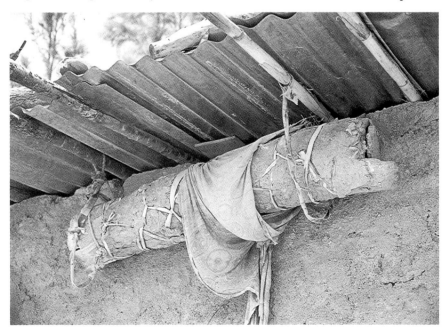

Figure 5.4 A log hive hung beneath the eaves of a building in Saudi Arabia to attract honeybee swarms.

such circumstances, many taboos have become associated with their use.

In parts of Kenya until recently, if not now, a man himself would not hang up in a tree the first hive he made, but this had to be done by his uncle; furthermore he must not have marital relations with his wife until two nights after a swarm had occupied it. In times of poor honey harvest, a village would sacrifice a goat to appease the spirits.

Taboos occurring in South Africa include forbidding a young man to eat honey when visiting his future father-in-law because his prospective bride might escape through his hands made slippery with honey! Once married, the bride may eat honey at her father's home but not at the house of her husband, in case doing so makes her behave like bees of a swarm that gorge themselves and leave home!

The next stage in the evolution of beekeeping could involve the transfer of occupied trap hives to near the home dwelling so they were conveniently placed and could be better protected. In other words a 'home apiary' was established. Probably, side by side with this step forward would be the collection of swarms in suitable containers which could be carried back to the apiary. For anybody who is well versed in obtaining honey from wild colonies, while wearing little or no protective clothing, the actual collection of a docile swarm would present few difficulties, once the idea had germinated that a swarm could be captured, transferred and would settle in its new home.

When a man had an established apiary of hives, however crude, he had effectively become a beekeeper, although no doubt honey hunting continued to be carried out simultaneously with trapping colonies and beekeeping as the opportunity presented itself.

Primitive hives and apiaries

Like the bee that now is blown
Honey-heavy on my hand,
From his toppling tansy-throne
In the green tempestuous land –
I'm in clover now, nor know
Who made honey long ago.

Edmund Blunden, 'Forefathers'

The nesting place for a honeybee colony must provide an upper surface from which bees can suspend their comb, darkness, shelter from wind, rain and extremes of temperature, and an entrance small enough to be defended.

The final stage in the transition from honey hunting to beekeeping is the construction of special containers or 'beehives' for the honeybee colonies. Probably the bees themselves first suggested to man the type of hive he might use. Swarms of bees readily occupy any man-made shelter of sufficient size to form a nest; large clay pots and wickerwork and woven baskets would seem eminently suitable to them, specially in the hot dry areas of the Middle East where trees and rock shelters are scarce.

So, many of the first beehives used by man were probably not designed as such but were adaptations of containers, of wood, clay or basketry, often used for other purposes, and were only slowly modified to suit the requirements of the beekeeper, if not the bees. Such hives were the only ones in existence until a few hundred years ago, and they can still be found in many parts of the world today. In many areas wickerwork, cane or plaited straw baskets have been used for general agricultural and household use since time immemorial. It is easy to envisage how these could be adapted, and weatherproofed by plastering the outside with mud, or animal dung, to become the predecessor of the first straw 'skep' hives. In some mountainous parts of Ethiopia, beekeepers are still using what is probably one of the crudest man-made hives of all, built of mud, cow dung and straw.

The original 'log hive' was undoubtedly of variable diameter and length but has tended to conform to local standards with the passage of time, or to have become modified as a bark cylinder. In some parts a log hive would be left vertical, as a tree trunk; in others it was laid horizontal, as a tree branch. Vertical log hives were traditional in northern Europe, and were still in use in North Carolina until a few

Figure 5.5 An apiary of traditional hives made from hollow trunks of date palm in the Sultanate of Oman.

years ago. The traditional hive of Oman is a horizontal hollowed-out trunk of a date palm of four hands' span in length, with a removable wooden plug at each end, one of which contains the entrance opening; 100 or more of these date log hives may be piled up together in a single apiary. Modern hives are only now being introduced for the first time.

A recent study in the Embu district of central Kenya portrays a type of beekeeping using log hives that has probably remained virtually unchanged for centuries. Although men and women share most of the productive work in the area, because of the hazardous journeys and tree climbing involved in beekeeping it is reserved solely for men. The division of labour is probably also linked with the beekeeper's pride in the skill, bravery and knowledge needed to carry out his tasks.

The hives are made from logs up to 150 cm long and 60 cm in diameter. After the wood inside has been chipped away, the ends are closed with round wooden plugs. A good hive will last 20–30 years. When construction is finished, hives are smeared with old honeycomb and sometimes fumigated with burning charcoal and honeycomb to make them attractive to swarms. They are then secured by sturdy fibres in the forks of tough branches, or even pegged in position. Trees that are easily climbed are preferred. When there is a possibility of animals such as genets or honey badgers pillaging the hives, they are suspended from the branches by stout cords. When more than one hive is placed in the same tree they all belong to the same man. One man may have up to about 50 hives.

As the hives are placed in position the beekeepers sing a traditional song, which may be translated as follows:

> I call all the bees to the bee-hive;
> Even those in my father's bee-hive;
> Even those on the hills;
> Even those in the valleys;
> And even those in the other plains,
> Bees bzz; Bees bzz; Bees bzz – in my bee-hive.

At intervals the beekeeper inspects his hives, to repair any damage done to them, eject any animals that may have nested in them, and if hives are unoccupied to add a 'bait' odour. When the hives to be inspected are some distance from the village, beekeepers may go in a group as added protection against wild beasts.

Collecting the honey is also often a communal affair. The beekeepers take with them sharp knives to cut out the combs, containers of goat skin or bark to take away the honeycomb, fibre ropes to raise and lower the containers and sometimes the hives, and bows and arrows for protection. It usually takes over an hour to collect the honeycomb from a hive, leaving behind brood comb so the colony may continue to survive and yield additional harvests. Honey collecting is usually done at night, darkness giving the beekeeper some measure of defence against angry bees. Even so, the beekeeper must blow smoke on the bees from burning brands and cut out the combs and lower them to an assistant, while he is often precariously perched on a branch in the dark, being stung by the bees, with dangerous animals lurking in the darkness below!

When honey has been collected from all the hives in an area, the beekeepers move away from the immediate vicinity before choosing a place in which to sleep for the remainder of the night, because with the coming of the dawn the occupants of the robbed hives are usually far from placid!

It is indicative of the esteem with which the prize is regarded that although women traditionally do all the carrying jobs, and it is beneath a man's dignity to do so, the man himself will carry home his honey harvest. The honey is put to many uses; it is prescribed to cure various ailments and has a significant part in important ceremonies including circumcision, initiation and marriage. But much of the honey collected goes into the production of honey beer, and it is no coincidence that many of the songs that accompany all aspects of beekeeping in the Embu area of Kenya are spiced with a ribald humour!

In parts of the world where trees are absent or scarce, clay pots, storage cylinders or pipes were adapted for use as beehives. In Iran, whole apiaries still consist of the traditional hives which are horizonatal clay cylinders, with the front plugs often beautifully decorated and glazed. The beekeeper frequently places sticks across the cavity at intervals to support the combs. The bees rear their brood in combs near the front of the hive and use combs further back for honey storage. To harvest the honey, the thin clay seal surrounding the rear plug is broken, the plug removed, and the combs of honey cut out with a long knife, leaving the brood undisturbed. The rear plug is then replaced and sealed with wet clay.

6 *Beekeeping in the ancient world*

Beekeeping in Ancient Egypt

He hath united the two lands,
He hath joined the Reed to the Bee.

Kahun papyrus

When considering beekeeping in the ancient civilisations of Egypt, Rome and Greece we have access for the first time to written evidence, and are able to replace conjecture, based largely on beekeeping by primitive or rural societies today, by recorded fact.

The earliest portrayal of beekeeping in Ancient Egypt was about 2500 BC in the Fifth Dynasty sun temple of Ne-user-re at Abusir, and shows that it was already well advanced. The scenes depicted show a beekeeper blowing smoke, probably from dried ox dung burning in a pottery vessel, at the colonies. These are in clay cylindrical hives, rather like those still present in Iran, Egypt and other parts of the Middle East today, piled on top of each other. Other figures can be seen filling jars with honeycomb, squeezing honey from the comb into other jars, and sealing vessels containing honey.

However, the bee was important in Egypt long before this time. It was used as a hieroglyph denoting the King of Lower Egypt from the First

Figure 6.1 *Top* Tracing of a relief from the temple of the Sun of Ne-user-re (Fifth Dynasty) at Abusir, Egypt, depicting beekeeping operations. Honey is being removed from clay hives on the extreme left and is being sealed into a honey pot on the right. *Bottom* Examples of stylised bees used as hieroglyphs in Ancient Egypt: (a) place name: 'Papyrus clump of the bee'; (b) honey; (c) beekeeper (after Hilda Ransome).

(a)　　　　**(b)**　　　　**(c)**

Dynasty to the Roman period, 4000 years later. The reason for its selection remains obscure. Perhaps the selection of a bee as a royal hieroglyph implied that the Ancient Egyptians knew of the existence of one special bee in each colony. Typically of Ancient Egyptian art, in the hieroglyph the bee is always in profile; the head, thorax and abdomen are always visible as are two wings, two antennae, and either three or commonly four legs.

The great magico-religious significance of bees and their products in Ancient Egypt cannot be better expressed than in the following contemporary legend:

> The god Re wept and the tears
> from his eyes fell on the ground
> and turned into a bee
> The bee made [his honeycomb]
> and busied himself
> with the flowers of every plant;
> and so wax was made
> and also honey
> out of the tears of the god Re.

Honey was thought to have strong healing powers, especially for respiratory ailments and eye diseases. The priests used honey, and cakes sweetened with honey, in many religious ceremonies, and honey together with goose flesh was fed to the sacred crocodiles. But honey was used for the dead as well as the living. Two jars bearing an inscription meaning 'honey of good quality' were found in the tomb of Tutankhamon. Embalmers also used wax to cover eyes, ears and nose during mummification. The coffin was made airtight with beeswax and the dead were sometimes preserved in honey. This was probably a traditional way of preserving bodies of important people in the Ancient Middle East. The deathbed wish of Alexander the Great that he should be buried in honey was subsequently granted, a 'white' honey being used for the purpose.

Beeswax was used in a variety of other ways: in cosmetics, for retaining the permanency of wig curls, as a protective covering for paintings, and as a binder for pigments used in painting. Model animals and 'magical' figures were also made of wax; its suitability for modelling led to it being used in the 'lost wax' *(cire perdu)* method of producing casts of metal statuettes and other metalwork in which the wax is replaced in the cast by molten metal.

Egypt was probably one of the first parts of the world where migratory beekeeping was practised. There is documentary evidence that donkeys were used to move hives in the Third Century BC, although migratory beekeeping was probably practised long before this. In Ancient Egypt, rafts were used to transport hives along the Nile and this was still so in

93

Figure 6.2 Gold pendant of two interlaced bees beneath a crown and holding between them a circular piece of comb taken from a cylinder hive; from the cemetery of Malia, Crete (7th century BC)

the 18th century. The migration started in October in Upper Egypt where flowering was early, and the hives were floated down a few miles at a time to Lower Egypt, keeping pace with the flowering of nectar- and pollen-producing plants, finally finishing their journey in Cairo (Memphis) in early February where the produce was sold.

Beekeeping in Ancient Greece

Smoke rolls and scarves in the grove
The mind of the hive thinks this is the end of everything.
Sylvia Plath, 'The Bee Meeting'

The Ancient Greeks probably learned much of the art of beekeeping from Egypt, and archaeological evidence indicates that hives similar to the horizontal clay cylinders of Egypt were used. Unfortunately, no contemporary illustrations of Greek hives are known.

Honey was used extensively in cookery and was often regarded as the key to a long life; certainly Pythagoras, in the 6th century BC, regularly consumed honey and lived to a great age. Honey was also sometimes used to preserve the bodies of Greeks who died far from home.

The period is rich in writings on bees and indicates that much was understood about life inside the bee colony. Hesiod, about 750 BC, knew that whereas the workers were busy in the field until sunset each day and then still produce 'the white and waxen combs', the 'slothful' drones that reap the benefit of their labours are fed and pampered by them 'within the close-roof'd hive'.

The natural history writings of Aristotle (384–322 BC) contain many original observations on bee behaviour, including the regurgitation of honey from the honey-stomachs of bees into cells. To make their observations, Aristotle and Hesiod must have been able to see bees at work on the combs, a situation impossible with the clay cylinder hive. This and other written evidence that relates to beekeeping practice indicates that the Ancient Greeks also possessed another type of hive which was to be of great significance in the development of beekeeping.

This was a woven basket hive, which was not inverted, but had the open end uppermost, covered with a roof, and was wider at the top than the bottom. In the 17th century, when it was first described by Sir George Wheeler in his book *A journey into Greece*, and probably much earlier, bars of wood were laid along the top of the basket and from these the bees suspended their combs. In these hives the bees do not attach their comb to the side walls to any great extent; the reason for this is probably connected with the angle of slope of the side walls of the hive, but it is not known for certain.

This hive had the advantage that the beekeeper could remove combs and so examine the condition of his colonies, could remove combs of honey for consumption but leave combs of brood behind, and also could make a new colony by placing some of the occupied combs in an empty hive.

In Ancient Greek and Roman civilisations the honeybee was regarded with much esteem and veneration. As in Egypt, honey cakes were considered a worthy offering to the gods and it was believed that honey formed part of their heavenly food. Bees, even if not of divine origin themselves, were at least often closely associated with the gods in legends. The following delightful legend is attributed to Anacreon:

Once Eros found a little bee
Sleeping upon a rose,
And was stung by it.
Hardly had he felt the finger
Of his little hand wounded,
He ran, he flew, sobbing
To the beautiful Kypris.
'Alas! alas! I am dying,
I have been bitten
By a little serpent
Who has however wings,
The country people call them bees.'
Then she spake, 'If the sting
Of the bee causes such pain,
Dost thou not think that it hurts
When thou, my son, woundest?

95

Beekeeping in Ancient Rome

So great is their love of flowers and pride in producing honey.

Virgil, *Georgics*

In the Ancient Roman Empire, beekeeping became an important and methodical pursuit, and much information about it has been passed down in the writings of Varro, Virgil, Columella and Pliny the Elder.

The hives were made of many materials including cork oak, fennel stems, and wickerwork, smeared with cow dung, and occasionally of

TROPHONIUS

Figure 6.3 Trophonius, the Greek high god responsible for safety and welfare, made use of his bees to guide those who sought his advice.

sawn pieces of wood, and were either rectangular or cylindrical. Extensions could be added to some of them to accept the honey in times of plenty. There were even hives of transparent lantern thorn so the activities of the occupants could be observed.

Many Roman farms had their apiaries. If the owner did not work the bees himself, he employed a beekeeper *(mellarius)* to do so. Varro stresses the value of regular inspection of hives, fumigation and cleaning, as well as determining the number of 'kings' present, the sex of the queen having not yet been determined. Columella described in detail how to extract honey from the combs, strain it through a wickerwork basket, and store it in earthenware vessels.

In Roman times, honey was as widely employed as sugar is now. It was used in cookery, sauces and dressings, and in preserving meat, fruit and vegetables. Romans liked to indulge themselves with many types of sweets *(dulcia)* whose main component was honey, and wines sweetened with honey were frequently drunk both at the beginning and at the end of a meal.

Virgil (70–19 BC) lived a quiet life near Naples among his lemon groves and hives. His writings on bees – his fourth *Georgic* is mostly devoted to them – are a curious mixture of fact and fiction. Some of his advice, such as that concerning the necessity of shade, shelter and a nearby water source when establishing an apiary, is very sound. In contrast it seems that he considered that the pollen loads of bees were small stones that served the bee as ballast during windy weather:

> And as when empty barks on billows float
> With sandy ballast, sailors trim the boat,
> So bees bear gravel stones, whose poising weight
> Steers thro' the whistling winds their steady flight.

However, Virgil's description of colony awakening and growth in the Spring is surely unsurpassed:

> . . . When the golden sun has driven winter to the ground
> And opened up all the leagues of the sky in summer light,
> Over the glades and woodlands at once they love to wander
> And suck the shiny flowers and delicate sip the streams.
> Sweet then is their strange delight
> As they cherish their children, their nestlings: then with craftsmanship they
> Hammer out the fresh wax and mould the tacky honey.
> Then, as you watch the swarm bursting from hive and heavenward
> Soaring, and floating there on the limpid air of summer –
> A vague and wind-warped column of cloud to your wondering eyes.

As in Ancient Greece, drones were derided for their laziness: 'Drones that laugh at honest toil, and reap where others sowed' (Virgil) and there were suggestions that beekeepers should seek to exterminate them. But Columella came to their rescue with the plea that 'Bounds should be set to cruelty'!

Migratory beekeeping was practised, and once again transport seems to have been mainly by water. Pliny the Elder described migratory beekeeping in a village called Hostilia on the banks of the river Po:

> The farmers of this settlement, when the flowers of the neighbourhood are over, place their hives on ships and take them during the night about five miles up the river. In the daytime the bees fly out and bring their booty to the ships, whose position is changed daily until it is noticed by the sinking of the ship lower in the water that the hives are full; they are then taken home and the honey extracted.

In many ways beekeeping reached a zenith under the 'Pax Romana'. With the uprisings and eruptions of the barbarians, the settled and safe times were no longer, and the culture of bees and beekeeping either ceased to spread or even receded. In many parts it did not revive and flourish again until the Middle Ages.

Beekeeping in Palestine and Arabia

> And after a time he [Samson] returned to take her, and he turned aside to see the carcase of the lion; and, behold, there was a swarm of bees and honey, in the carcase of the lion.
> And he took thereof in his hands, and went on eating, and came to his father and mother, and he gave them, and they did eat.   *Judges 14*, 8–9

In the Bible, Palestine is often referred to as 'a land flowing with milk and honey' (*Exodus 3*, 8), but it is impossible to determine whether this alludes to beekeeping or merely gathering honey from wild colonies which probably abounded in the caves and crevices. Certainly there were wild colonies, as we find references to 'honey from the rocks' (*Psalms 81*, 16), 'honey in the carcase of the lion' (*Judges 14*, 8) and honeycomb dropping onto the floor of a wood (*Samuel I 14*, 26). On the other hand, we find that John the Baptist, when in the wilderness, ate 'wild honey' (*Matthew 3*, 4) which might be taken to imply that this was different from 'domesticated' honey.

Whatever the case, honey was certainly appreciated; the judgements of the Lord were 'sweeter also than honey and honeycomb' (*Psalms 19*, 10) and his words were 'sweeter than honey to my mouth' (*Psalms 119*, 103). Debôrah (Bee) appears to have been a favoured female name (*Genesis 35*, 8; *Judges 4*, 5). Honey from Palestine was exported to Tyre (*Genesis 27*, 17), and was among the gifts sent by Jacob to the governor of Egypt (*Genesis 43*, 11):

He sent a present meet –
Nuts, spices, balm, and luscious fruits,
A little honey sweet.

Bernard Fell

However, there are implications that the collection of honey was not always easy; the enemies of the Lord are referred to as having 'compassed me about like bees' (*Psalms 118*, 12) and Amorites as having attacked 'and chased you, as bees do' (*Deuteronomy 1*, 44).

According to Biblical sources, honey could have been among the first and last food that Jesus Christ ate on Earth. Isaiah, prophesying the birth of Christ, writes: 'Behold, a virgin shall conceive, and bear a son, and shall call his name Immanuel. Butter and honey shall he eat, that he may know to refuse the evil, and choose the good' (*Isaiah 7*, 14–15). After Christ's resurrection and just before his ascent into heaven he asked, 'Have ye here any meat? And they gave him a piece of a broiled fish, and of an honeycomb. And he took it, and did eat before them' (*Luke 24*, 42).

Certainly colonies of bees were being kept in hives during the lifetime of Muhammad the Prophet (AD 571–632), who founded the Muslim religion. Chapter 16 of the Holy Koran, which is entitled 'The Bee', contains the following passages:

> Your Lord inspired the bee, saying 'Build your homes in the mountains, in the trees, and in the hives which men shall make for you. Feed on every kind of fruit and follow the trodden paths of your Lord'.
> From its belly comes forth a fluid of many hues, a medicinal drink for men. Surely in this there is a sign for those who would give thought.

Muhammad is on record as saying 'Honey is a remedy for every illness, and the Koran is a remedy for all illness of the mind, therefore I recommend to you both remedies, the Koran and honey'. Small wonder that the bee is held in high esteem throughout the Arab world, and numerous legends, customs and beliefs have been associated with it.

Tradition has it that the bee once complained to the Prophet that man ate the food of its children and requested that after it had stung a man God should 'let him die'. However, by mistake the bee said 'let me die' and the request was granted!

Beekeeping in Arabia 2000 years ago was probably much as it still is in this century, the colonies being kept in hollow logs of acacia or date palm. Honey hunting is still practised in the south of the peninsular much as the explorer C. M. Doughty recorded it in 1926 for a tribe of mountain dwellers 'who are very long-lived and of marvellous vigour in their extreme age, as they are nourished on venison and wild honey'.

Despite the long tradition of beekeeping in Arabia, much of the basic

Figure 6.4 Selling liquid honey in the market of Al Hamra in the Sultanate of Oman. The potential buyer is testing its viscosity.

biology is still misunderstood by many beekeepers, who tend to relate the social organisation of a honeybee colony to their own tribal structure. In Yemen, tradition has it that the queen is father of the colony who leads an army of soldiers (workers) with swords to sting with; the bee women are larger and do not sting (drones).

In parts of rural Oman where beekeeping is practised with the little honeybee, *Apis florea*, the queen is the 'sheik', the workers are the 'people', and the drones being black are called 'slaves'. Supposedly, the

Figure 6.5 Beekeeping with *Apis florea* in the Sultanate of Oman. The colony is kept in the crude 'shelter' behind the comb.

'people' and 'slaves' each contain both sexes and reproduce among themselves but do not interbreed.

Beekeeping with *Apis florea* is probably practised more in the Sultanate of Oman than elsewhere, but has been described only recently. A beekeeper seeks for colonies in mountain caves, bushes or trees, and on finding one moves it from its natural nesting place to near his home, where it is both conveniently located and probably nearer to sources of forage in the irrigated land surrounding his village. The upper area of comb containing the honey is cut away from the remainder, which is gripped near the top between two parts of a split piece of date stem whose ends are tightly bound so the comb cannot slip out. The ends of the stick are then rested in convenient supports in a lime tree or date palm, or in an artificial cave specially constructed to hold it. As brood emerges from cells in the upper part of the comb, the bees lengthen them to receive honey stores, and extend the comb and brood rearing below, so that in favourable conditions the colony will soon produce another 'honey crop'.

7 *Evolution of beekeeping in Europe*

Beekeeping in Medieval Britain and Europe

> . . . we have rather
> chosen to fill our hives with honey and wax; thus
> furnishing mankind with the two noblest of things,
> which are sweetness and light.
>
> Dean Swift, 'Battle of the Books'

When the Romans invaded Britain the dome-shaped hive was of entwined willow or hazel twigs plastered inside and out with cow dung; these types of hive survived in parts of Britain until the 18th century, and locally they were sometimes more common than straw skeps.

In Roman Britain, various methods were used to locate wild colonies. Bees collecting water were marked with ochre to determine the duration of their absence from the water source and so whether their nest was likely to be nearby. Bees were also enticed into hollow reeds containing honey, and then released one at a time so that the direction of their flight could be followed until the nest was discovered.

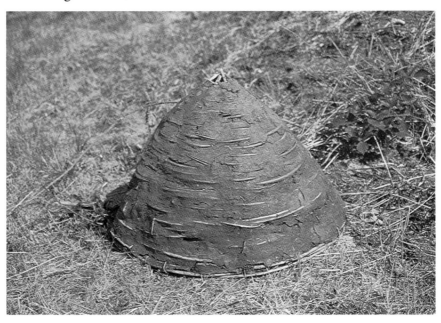

Figure 7.1
Reconstruction of an old wattle and daub hive.

Many Roman citizens in Britain were bee owners, but few worked the bees themselves and the task of doing so was undertaken by British slaves. Probably, this is one reason why beekeeping remained virtually unchanged in Britain throughout the Roman occupation. Indeed it did so for some hundreds of years thereafter.

The ancient laws of England, Wales and Ireland frequently referred to bees and honey. Fortunately the ancient laws of Ireland, or the 'Senchus Mor', which were handed down verbally for many centuries, were put into writing by the instigation of St Patrick about AD 440. These writings are rich in information about beekeeping in Ireland at the time.

The honey storage vessels, and by implication the honey crops, of Ireland were large; the three types of storage vessel were classified according to whether a man could raise it over his head, up to his chest, or up to his waist, when it was full of honey.

Long before the pollinating value of bees was understood, it was thought that their visits damaged fruits and flowers. Because of this supposedly obnoxious habit bees were only supposed to forage a distance from their hives equivalent to the sound that a bell or cock's crow would carry; if this distance was exceeded the owner of the land on which the trespass was occurring was entitled to a forfeit of a swarm of bees or some fruit, or failing this he was entitled to capture and keep the trespassing bees!

If a bee killed or maimed an animal or man, it was sometimes necessary to draw lots to decide whose hive the bee had come from, and the loser paid a heavy fine. However, the fine was less if the offending party had killed the bee that stung him.

In Saxon times, beekeeping must have been extensive to have produced the vast quantity of the much favoured mead that was drunk. The worshippers of Odin and Thor envisaged a paradise in which the nights were spent drinking mead which beautiful virgins presented to them in the skulls of their enemies. As Penrose expressed it in his 'Carousal of Odin':

Fill the honey'd bev'rage high,
Fill the skulls, 'tis Odin's cry!

The word 'honeymoon' is derived from the ancient custom of presenting newlyweds with mead to drink on each of the first 30 days after their marriage. It is perhaps a tribute to mead drinking that in Anglo-Saxon society the beekeeper (or *beo-ceorl*) was aligned with the swineherd in the lowest category of free men! Judging by the repeated mentions of bees, colonies, honey and wax in the *Domesday book*, beekeeping continued to flourish under the Normans in the 11th century.

As the huge forests of northern and central Europe were cleared, and the land subdivided, the owner marked any tree containing wild colonies to claim his right to the honey crop. In 1217, the Charter of Henry III of England declared that 'Every Freeman . . . shall likewise have the honey which shall be found in his woods'. At a later stage, the beekeeper hollowed out the tree-trunk, often near its top, to make a suitable nest for bees to occupy. The old Russian word for bee man is '*drevolazecu*', meaning tree climber. Later there followed the usual progressive evolutionary pattern of suspending hollow logs in the trees to collect swarms, and finally keeping the logs, usually vertically, in a clearing on the forest floor, or near to the beekeeper's dwelling.

Throughout the centuries, beeswax was used in producing models, seals, writing tablets, cosmetics, medicines and candles. The last-mentioned were burned extensively in magical and religious ceremonies. Beekeeping in central Europe received a great impetus from the spread of Christianity and the need for beeswax to produce the candles used by the churches. Beekeepers had their own patron saint in St Ambrose, who is frequently represented in painting or sculpture with a beehive or a bee skep.

Every monastery and abbey had its own apiary, a tradition often continued to this day, and many of the peasants who worked or rented Church land also kept bees, and so could pay part of their yearly rent in wax.

The Church's reverence for bees and beeswax was in some ways related to a misconception of the bees' method of reproduction; a paschal 5th century hymn from Italy extols the virtues of bees 'who produce posterity, rejoice in offspring, yet retain their virginity'. The white wax of the candle was also supposed to represent the spotless body

Figure 7.2 An apiary of vertical 'log' hives (16th century). The beekeeper is tanging the bees by banging the stick on the metal basin. This was supposed to make the swarm settle.

of Jesus Christ and the flame of the candle to represent the 'light of the world'. The alternative to the superior wax candles were those of tallow, or animal fats, which, when burned, gave a most unpleasant smell, quite unsuited to Holy Places.

Candles were needed not only for church altars but by the aristocracy for measuring time. The demand led King Alfred of England to decree that '. . . every beekeeper must announce the issue of a swarm by ringing bells or clashing metals so that it might be followed and captured'. Indeed, so valuable was wax that Hywel the Good of Wales ruled that the King's chamberlain had the right to as much wax as he could bite from the end of a wax taper.

Because of the link between the spread of Christianity and beekeeping, many of the myths surrounding beekeeping had a religious flavour. Anybody who started beekeeping should do so with three hives, the sacred number; bees should not be purchased or moved on a Friday; the newly born was regarded as a 'spirit' until honey was smeared on its mouth.

Like the Muslims, the Christians also had a story to explain why a bee dies after it has stung. It originated in Nièvre, France. When God was distributing gifts, the bees asked for a silver hive and that their stings might be fatal. God was so angry at their presumption that he ordered them to inhabit hives of straw or osier covered with cow dung and furthermore that every bee that stings shall die.

One custom that originated in the Middle Ages and is still practised to this day is 'telling the bees' when their master dies, otherwise they might leave to look for him. In fact, nobody liked to buy a dead man's bees in case they did so. One solution to the problem was to tie a piece of the dead man's clothing to each hive so that the bees still thought him alive. Likewise, bees must be informed of other important events such as marriage. In 'The Bee-Boy's Song', Rudyard Kipling echoes this early tradition:

A maiden in her glory,
Upon her wedding-day,
Must tell her Bees the story,
Or else they'll fly away.

Bees also possessed magical qualities that might lead to romance; apparently it helped a maiden to find a partner at a dance if she carried a piece of twig on which a swarm had settled.

A folk tale from Austria and neighbouring areas attempts to explain why honeybees cannot obtain nectar from red clover. It relates that when God created bees he ordered that for 6 days they should visit the flowers but on the seventh day they should rest. But the bees ignored him and worked unceasingly day after day, and in particular they visited

red clover flowers from which they obtained the best honey. As a punishment, God made the nectar of red clover inaccessible to them.

Fortunately, the link between Christianity and beekeeping had the great advantage that bees and hives were illustrated in many of the illuminated manuscripts produced by the monasteries. Many depict bees in flowers or flying from them back to the hives.

The production of beeswax and honey was of course linked, so that demand for beeswax also resulted in more honey. But even though honey was the only form of sweetening until sugar became available from sugar cane and sugar beet, it was not used extensively for cooking, and sugar consumption in Medieval Europe remained only a fraction of what it is today.

Although in early days candles were produced by monks and servants, in the 12th century the wax chandlers had emerged as specialised tradesmen and had organised themselves into guilds. Their business was to process beeswax and to make and sell candles and other products, and perhaps above all to ensure the maintenance of high quality products. To the present day, the City of London Guild of Wax Chandlers, although no longer practising their medieval craft, still give thanks with the traditional grace:

> For thy creature the Bee,
> The Wax and the Honey
> We thank thee, O Lord.
> By the light of all men,
> Christ Jesus our King,
> May this food now be blessed. Amen.

Bees and warfare

The bee that hath honey in her mouth, hath a sting in her tail.

John Lyly, 'Euphues'

Man has not only involved the bee in his religious life but also in his wars. Because the bee can be easily provoked, soldiers have tried to use its ferocity against enemies.

In the Middle Ages, both attacking and besieging forces hurled beehives among their foes, and this sometimes had the desired effect of causing surrender or retreat. An army of Danes and Norwegians who were besieging the English city of Chester in AD 908 could not be dissuaded from undermining the fortifications until the defenders collected all the city's beehives and hurled them down at the foe. One military machine used in the early 14th century was in the form of a windmill, and straw hives were propelled from the ends of the sails when they were rapidly revolved.

It is recorded that, in the American Civil War, a Union detachment

Figure 7.4 The besieged of Kissingen, Bavaria, defending themselves by throwing beehives at the attacking force (17th century).

was advancing through an apiary, when Confederate cannon smashed the hives, roused the bees and initiated a Union retreat.

In World Wars I and II, and in Vietnam, beehives were attached to trip wires to serve as booby traps. For example, in East Africa in 1914, the Germans hid numerous hives in dense bush and attached trip wires to the hive covers, so that as the British troops advanced they roused the bees and were severely stung; needless to say, being British, they did *not* retreat!

Beekeeping in Britain in the 17th and 18th centuries

When like the Bee, tolling from every flower
The virtuous sweets;
Our thighs packed with wax, our mouths with honey,
We bring it to the Hive; and, like the Bees,
Are murdered for our pains.

William Shakespeare, *Henry IV*

Figure 7.5 A swarm being brushed into a skep hive (17th century).

Following the Reformation, and the dissolution of the monasteries in 1537 in England, the demand for beeswax and altar candles diminished greatly. Furthermore, increasing imports of French wines lessened the demand for home-produced mead. Finally, in common with the rest of Europe, production of sugar from cane and beet reduced the demand for honey. However, despite all this there remained a great and sustained interest in the 'science' and practice of beekeeping and in the bees themselves.

Beekeeping still depended very much on the production and capture of swarms and, to encourage swarming, the internal cavity of the straw basket hive or 'skep' was kept small. In spring and early summer the beekeeper kept a close vigilance on his colonies so he could capture any swarms that emerged and use them to populate his empty hives. At the end of the summer season he selected some of his colonies for the following year and fed them if necessary, and took honey from the rest.

Writings from a manuscript by John Evelyn in about 1680 describe current beekeeping practices, and are fascinating not only in revealing contemporary methods but also contemporary knowledge of colony organisation, neither of which had seen much improvement for many years. The following passages are extracted from this manuscript:

The method to Govern Bees is as follows.

1. On the buying them choose the most weightiest hives, but if the party that looked to them be dead, they will not thrive with a succeeding master which is mysterious.

2. The best way of preserving them is to get good hives and cover them with a cap of small or chopped hay and cow dung tempered over them, or with small hay and an earthen pan made fit for the top of the hive, which will keep them from the scorching heat of summer and from the severe frosts in winter, and also keep mice from eating into the crown of the hive, which they are subject to, when they stand under a painthouse without such hard caps.

3. Every hive must have a distinct forme to stand upon, otherwise the Bees of one hive will rob the other.

4. They must be placed against the South sun, a little declining from the East, otherwise the Bees will fly out too early and be subject to the mischief of cold Dews.

5. In April they gather not honey but Bee bread for their young (increas) and therefore must be fed, about 5 or 6 a clock in the evening, if you feed them in the morning they will be lazy and not work.

6. At Michaelmas examine which bees to keep and which to destroy. Those hives that weigh about 30 pound, that is hive, Bees and honey, is a good hive to keep, those under that weight are not fit to keep. For a poor or small

swarm will require more feeding and tendance than a great swarm; the reason is, that a hive full of Bees keeps a heat within which is nourishing; for the stomach requires least meat in hot weather. If a hive weigh 50 or 60 pound then take it, being well stored with honey and perhaps too old to keep.

If as sometimes they fight, flight dust among them, sweet water or Beer which will make them all smell alike and reconcile them. The punctures and stinging of Bees is cured by their own honey, by juice of Malows, by cow dung mixed with vinegar.

John Evelyn had carefully observed the process of swarming:

For being too full and numerous, they send forth new *Colonies*; but first they who are assigned for the expedition resort together about the Hive 'till their King having found fit a place for their *Rendez-vous* first lights himself. Then immediately followed with innumerable numbers pitching their camp round about their Royal General they hang together, till certain scouts which before they had sent forth *tanquam exploratores* bring them tidings of a convenient quarter. Which notice he gives them by a certain touch which he imparts to the out guards that by a kind of shivering motion communicate it to the whole swarm and centre bees in a moment; at which signal they dissolve the populous and moving cone and fly immediately to the place, their King leading them in front.

Figure 7.6 The beekeeper has removed the cover from a 'skep' hive and is puffing smoke in the entrance to pacify the bees. 'Skep' hives were common in Europe until this century.

To obtain honey from 'skep' hives the bees were usually killed with fumes of burning sulphur. At the end of the summer season, skeps of medium weight were selected for surviving the winter and providing next year's harvest and swarms to fill empty hives, and the honey was removed from the remainder.

There can hardly be a better or more amusing description of taking honey from a skep hive than that made by a Chepstow housewife on 30 September 1796:

> Sarah did dig a big hole in the ground for each skep, wherein we did put a sulfur paper which we did set alight, and put the skep of bees on the top, the smell of the sulfur do kill the bees, and so we do get the honey there from. It do grieve me to kill the poor things, being such a waste of good bees, to lie in a great heap at the bottom of the hole when the skep be took off it, but we do want the honey, using a great lot in the house for divers times. Carter's wife did fall backwards and sat in a skep of bees, which did make a great buzzing and did send her youping out of the garden, at which Sarah did laff so heartily to see carter's wife holding up her gown while jumping over the cabbidges, that she did nearly do the same thing, at which I quite helpless to reprove her, laffing myself at the carter's wife spindly legs abobbing up and down among the vegetables. She back anon, with a mighty big nose where a bee had sat on it, and we to the out house with the honey skeps, there to leave them till sure all the bees be gone.
>
> We shall break the honey combs up and hang it up in a clean cotton bag to run it through then we shall strain it divers times and when clear put the pots reddie to use. The wax we do boil many times till it be a nice yaller colour and no bits of black in it, when it can be stored for use for the polishing and harness cleaning.

Much effort was put into finding means of removing honey without killing the bees. Extensions were added above or below the skeps, to give chambers in which honey was stored but the queen was unlikely to be present and lay eggs, so that they, complete with the brood-free honeycombs the bees built in them, could be removed at harvest time without destroying the colony.

Even when the destruction of the brood and comb was unavoidable, attempts were made to save the bees by a process known as 'driving the bees'. The hive whose honey was to be taken was inverted and another hive placed on top of it; the walls of the lower hive were 'drummed', causing the bees to move upward and join the colony above. Sometimes several colonies were driven into the same hive, the surviving queen heading a populous colony that readily swarmed and restocked the empty hives the following spring.

Although most hives were of straw and were sulphured in this way, an array of wooden types of hive was also available, although much more expensive.

Sir Christopher Wren produced a sketch of an octagonal hive, which **111** became popular and was used by Samuel Pepys, among others. At about the same time, glass windows were cut into the sides of hives so the activities of the occupants could be observed. A passage in Pepys's *Diary* of 1665 reads: 'After dinner to Mr Evelyn's; he being abroad, we walked in his garden, and a lovely noble ground he hath indeed. And among other rarities a hive of bees, so as being hived in glass, you may see the bees making their honey and comb mighty pleasantly.'

One hive, designed by the Scot, Robert Kerr (1755–1840) and named after his home town of Stewarton, deserves special mention. It consists of a tier of octagonal boxes, each with fixed wooden parallel bars from which the combs are suspended, the intervening spaces having wooden slides so that access of the bees to the boxes can be regulated. At the end of the season the boxes were sold complete with their comb and honey.

A number of old dwellings in the British Isles can be found with recesses made in their walls, or in the walls of their gardens, to accommodate beehives. These dwellings include farms, cottages and manor houses dating back to the 15th century.

Figure 7.7
Reconstruction of the Stewarton octagonal hive.

The recesses, or 'boles', are constructed of many different building *Britain in the 17th and* materials, and are a variety of sizes and shapes. The older bee boles tend *18th centuries* to be smaller, in association with the small size of the skep hives then used. Usually the bee boles are rectangular, but sometimes the tops are gabled or rounded. Most face south.

Undoubtedly, bee boles sheltered the perishable hives from rain, and would be particularly valuable in the wetter parts of the country. Certainly they are the oldest relics of beekeeping in Britain.

8 *History of beekeeping in America*

Honey from stingless bees

Sugar in the gourd and honey in the horn,
I never was so happy since the hour I was born.

Anonymous, c. 1800

The true honeybees (genus *Apis*) are not indigenous to America; until the arrival of *Apis* spp. with European settlers in the 16th and 17th

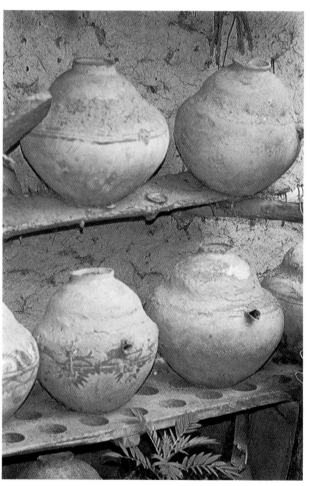

Figure 8.1 Clay pots used by peasant beekeepers for housing meliponine colonies in Mexico (photo by R. Darchen).

centuries, stingless bees provided almost the sole means of sweetening for the American continent.

Honey from stingless bees

As with the true honeybees, hunting stingless bee colonies probably occurred for many centuries before beekeeping with them began, and the use of trap hives to collect swarms was no doubt an intermediate step. But since the beginning of the 19th century, and probably earlier, it has been the practice of Mexican beekeepers to start new stingless bee colonies with bees and brood removed from established ones.

In Central and South America, beekeeping with stingless bees was well established before the Spaniards arrived in the 16th century. The colonies were commonly kept in dried gourds, hollow logs or cylindrical earthenware pots; the latter were blocked with circular doors at either end and each had an entrance hole half way along its length.

The Ancient Maya of Yucatán, in Central America, were the most important honey producers. When Bishop Fray Diego de Landa visited Yucatán in the middle of the 16th century, he reported that the land abounded in honey that was used for sweetening and for making mead into which an alkaloid-yielding bark was steeped. The festival of the honey god, Ah-Mucencab, occurred during the fifth month of the

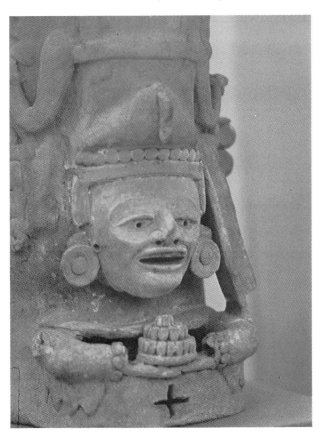

Figure 8.2 The Mayan honey god, Ah-Mucencab, Museum de Méride. Under the face is a cluster of meliponine honeypots.

Mayan calendar. Its purpose was to persuade the god to send an abundance of flowers for the bees, but it also provided an opportunity for the participants to consume liberal quantities of mead. Some of the few remaining Mayan manuscripts of the pre-Columbian period contain hieroglyphs and figures depicting bees, comb and vessels for storing honey.

Although not more than about 2 kg of honey could be squeezed from the comb of a stingless bee colony, a considerable amount of honey was harvested by the beekeepers, and in the early 16th century Hernando Cortés and his conquistadores reported that honey and beeswax were to be purchased in the Aztec markets. Both the Maya and the Aztecs imposed a tribute of honey on the people of subservient tribes. Indeed, sometimes the only occupations which they allowed them to retain were pot making and beekeeping.

When the true honeybees were eventually introduced into Central and South America from North America, they tended to replace the stingless bees as honey producers. But beekeeping with stingless bees is still practised in parts of Central and South America today. Stingless bees could be important pollinators of many tropical crops, although evidence is generally lacking. Certainly, in the absence of more information, it is provident to conserve existing colonies.

Introduction of beekeeping into North America

Whereso'er they move, before them
Swarms the stinging fly, the Ahmo,
Swarms the Bee, the honey-maker;
Whereso'er they tread, beneath them
Springs a flower unknown among us,
Springs the White Man's Foot in blossom.

H. W. Longfellow, 'Hiawatha'

Honeybee colonies were taken in straw skeps to North America by settlers from Europe in the 17th century. The first report of their successful establishment came from Virginia in 1622, followed by Massachusetts in 1638. We have little idea as to how many colonies survived the sea voyage to the eastern coast. Their survival on arrival in North America would no doubt depend on the season of the year and the time available to hoard food before winter set in.

However, once established many swarms colonised natural nesting sites and moved ahead of the settlers. As the lines from 'Hiawatha' indicate, the arrival of the bee, or White Man's Fly, and the White Man's Foot as Red Indians named 'white clover', was taken to herald the arrival of the white man himself. Although few Indians other than those of the

Cherokee tribe kept bees themselves, they soon learned that by watching the line of flight of the bees they could discover the nests of wild colonies and take the honey.

Beekeeping was well established in Virginia and Massachusetts by the middle of the 17th century, reached Florida in 1763, Kentucky in 1793 and was probably practised throughout the eastern part of the USA by 1800, so providing the settlers with beeswax and honey, and pollinating their crops. Most of the colonies were kept in crude plank hives or hollowed tree trunks.

A Russian monk took honeybees to Alaska in 1809 and from Alaska bees were taken to California in 1830. Some hives were also carried overland on the backs of covered wagons to the western coast in the mid 19th century, soon after the great gold rush had begun. There are reports that in California in 1853 these hives sold for $111. Another route by which bees reached California was by ship to the Isthmus of Panama, overland to the Pacific Ocean and then by ship for the rest of the journey. From California, the honeybee soon spread north to British Columbia.

The medicinal powers of honey and bee stings were thought to be great in the pioneer days, and still have some staunch advocates today. Fantastic tales of bees and honey production came to be told, especially from Texas.

The age-old custom of 'telling the bees' when their master died was imported from Europe. J. G. Whittier, the 19th century New England poet, was inspired to write:

Just the same as a month before,
The house and the trees,
The barn's brown gable, the vine by the door,
Nothing changed but the hive of bees.

Before them, under the garden wall,
Forward and back
Went drearily singing the chore-girl small,
Draping each hive with a shred of black.

Trembling I listened, the summer sun
Had the chill of snow;
For I knew she was telling the bees of one
Gone on the journey we all must go!

The importance of the honeybee to man is readily acknowledged in North America today. It is the 'State Insect' of Arkansas, Georgia, Nebraska, New Jersey, North Carolina and Michigan; Utah has a beehive in the centre of its state seal.

117

9 *Advances in knowledge and techniques*

Important scientific discoveries

> The human race, in its intellectual life, is organised like the bees: the masculine soul is a worker, sexually atrophied, and essentially dedicated to impersonal and universal arts; the feminine is a queen, infinitely fertile, omnipresent in its brooding industry, but passive and abounding in intuitions without method and passions without justice.
>
> George Santayana, *The Life of Reason*

For many years, the 'leader' of the bee colony was thought of as a 'king'; it was not until 1586 that Luis Méndez de Torres of Spain discovered that the 'queen' was a female and observed her laying eggs.

This was followed in 1609 by an important treatise, *The feminine monarchie,* by Charles Butler of England, who confirmed that the queen was female and mother of the colony. His preface proclaims, 'We must not call the Queen "Rex", the Bee-state is an Amazonian or feminine Kingdom'. Charles Butler was also the first to realise that the 'drones' were male bees. As he was the Rector of Wooton, the following passage comes as no surprise: 'If thou wilt have the favour of the bees that they sting thee not, thou must avoid such things as offend them; thou must not be unchaste and uncleanly; for impurities and skittishness (themselves being most chaste and neat) they utterly abhor'. He listed the following as enemies of the bee: the mouse, woodpecker, sparrow, swallow, hornet, wasp, moth, snail, emmet, spider, toad and frog. He prescribed some quaint remedies: for example, 'for the mouse, sometimes tie a cat to the hive stool'. Butler was prolific and versatile; he also published books on logic, music, English grammar and the marriage of cousins.

In 1637, Richard Remannt published *A discourse or historie of bees* in which he understood that drones were produced at the pleasure of the bees and advocated the use of drone traps made of osier. He also recognised the workers as female, and so the sexes of the different castes had finally all been discovered. These findings were confirmed by the great Dutch naturalist Jan Swammerdam (1637–1685).

However, it was many years before they were accepted. As late as

118

1679, Moses Rusden, who was beemaster to Charles II of England, was so intent on upholding the divine right of kings that he would not admit that the Royal Bees were female or that the drones were male, but wrote instead of the king, generals and soldiers in the beehive. He allowed that 'workers' were female but was greatly puzzled over the functions of drones.

The first account of the queen's mating was given by Anton Janscha of Slovenia in 1771, but the foundations of our present knowledge of the bee colony were laid in 1792 by Francois Huber, the blind Swiss scientist who was fortunate to have a superb and trusted observer in his assistant Francis Burnens. His discoveries, aided by the use of a special hive in which the combs were in wooden frames hinged together like the pages of a book, paved the way for an understanding of the influence of the queen in the colony, queen rearing and fertilisation, temperature regulation and colony defence.

In the same year, 1792, John Hunter in England observed that 'during severe weather bees retain their warmth by clustering, and swarming bees always have full crops'. He also described bee communication dances: 'We very often see some of the bees wagging their belly, as if tickled, running round, and to and fro, for only a little way, followed by one or two other bees as if examining them'.

The 19th century

> Here is my honey-machine,
> It will work without thinking,
> Opening, in spring like an industrious virgin.
>
> Sylvia Plath, 'Stings'

The proliferation of hive types reached its zenith in the 19th century. Some were very elaborate and were associated with special systems of beekeeping. These and early hives often had wooden top bars or complete wooden frames to hold the bees' combs. Even in 1686, a John Whitehall of Staffordshire, England, had built himself square brick hives containing wooden frames. But the wooden frames in these hives became attached to the walls of the hive with comb or propolis and were extremely difficult to remove.

Similarly, the hives with wooden top bars only had the advantage that the bees suspended their combs from them rather than from the hive roof, but suffered from the disadvantage that the bees often attached the comb to the side walls of the hive, and to remove a comb the beekeeper had to cut it free.

A major exception was a traditional Greek hive already referred to, and seen and described by Sir George Wheeler in 1682 when he visited

Figure 9.1 A 19th century beekeeper who has acquired a moveable frame hive (after Jenkins).

some of the monastries. This was a woven basket hive, wider at the top than the bottom. The combs suspended from the top bars hung free and could be lifted out and examined. In the spring it was common practice to double the number of colonies that had survived the winter by removing half the combs from each hive and putting them in an empty one.

It has been supposed that the slope of the side walls of these hives discourages bees from attaching comb to them. There is some evidence to support this, but more investigations are necessary. Hives similar in principle to these traditional hives of Greece have recently been used in beekeeping development programmes in East Africa, Nepal and elsewhere.

However, it was not until the middle of the 19th century that a solution was found to the major problem of providing combs in frames which could easily be removed to inspect and manipulate the colony. There is a certain width of space (about ¼ in or 6 mm) through which a bee can readily pass but which she will not fill either with wax comb or propolis. This space has become known as the 'bee space'.

It was first discovered in 1851 by the Rev. L. L. Langstroth, who was an amateur beekeeper in Pennsylvania, USA. He relates how, returning late in the afternoon from his apiary, he was pondering as to:

120   how I could get rid of the disagreeable necessity of cutting the attachments of the combs from the walls of the hives . . . and in a moment the suspended

moveable frames, kept at a suitable distance from each other and the case containing them, came into being. Seeing by intuition, as it were, the end from the beginning, I could scarcely refrain from shouting out my 'Eureka!' in the open streets.

Langstroth used his discovery to devise a hive, which now bears his name and is used world wide, in which the frames are separated from each other and from the walls of the hive by a bee space, and so are not joined together and can be removed at will.

The Rev. Langstroth did not begin beekeeping until he was 28 years old, when he knew little or nothing about bees; undoubtedly his fresh outlook, combined with his keen powers of observation, facilitated his discovery.

Having made this fundamental advance, many others were possible, both at the commercial and scientific fronts; indeed Langstroth's discovery formed the basis of modern beekeeping throughout the world.

One of the earliest inventions that followed was the provision by Johannes Mehring of Germany in 1857 of what has become known to beekeepers as 'wax foundation'. These are sheets of wax that are impressed with the hexagonal pattern of bee cells. Bees accept the hexagons as the bases of their cells, and build up the walls on them, so producing good combs of even quality.

The wax foundation usually has thin wires embedded in it, which provide the resulting comb with sufficient strength to withstand the centrifugal force of the honey extractor invented by Major F. Hruschka of Austria in 1865 to spin honey out of the cells.

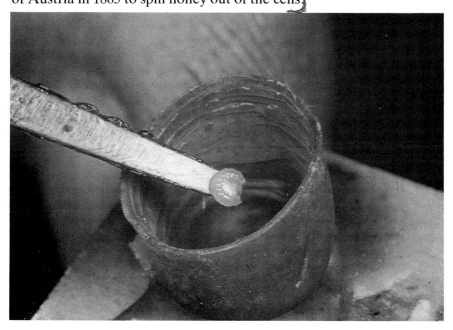

Figure 9.2 Transferring young worker larvae into an artificial queen cell.

Figure 9.3 Queen cells each containing a queen pupa. Beekeepers are able to manipulate colonies so they rear new queens to replace ones that are growing old.

In the same year, Abbé Collin of France produced a 'queen excluder'. This is basically a sheet of perforated metal, or a grid of wires with apertures of sufficient width to allow the workers, but not the queen, to pass. The queen excluder can be used to confine the queen, and hence brood rearing, to one or two chambers of the hive.

In 1877, T. F. Bingham of the USA invented the bellows smoker which provides a gentle cloud of smoke rather than the torrent of smoke used since early times to drive bees from the hive. In 1891, E. C. Porter, also of the USA, invented a 'bee escape' which allows bees to pass through it in one direction only, and so can be used effectively to remove bees from the honey chambers of hives prior to taking away the combs of honey.

All these 19th century inventions facilitated the production of good, clean honey.

In modern beekeeping practices, the production of new queens is no longer left to chance, but selected larvae are carefully lifted from their cells, transferred to 'artificial queen cups' and introduced to a colony that has been specially prepared to receive them, where they are reared to maturity. The methods currently employed are much the same as methods developed towards the end of the 19th century, and especially to those of G. M. Doolittle of the USA. Much progress has now been made in selecting genetic stock with desirable characteristics.

122

The present situation

Honey and beeswax production today

> Oh! yet
> Stands the church clock at ten to three
> And is there honey still for tea?
> Rupert Brooke, 'The Old Vicarage, Granchester'

Although all moveable-frame hives developed during this century employ the 'bee space' principle, many are of a different size from the 'Langstroth' hive and use a different size of frame. Some are not for honey production at all, but for use in rearing or in mating queens. Those used for queen mating may be very small, as they need to contain only sufficient bees to care for and protect the queen just before and after her mating flight. They may hold only two or three combs of normal size, or sometimes ones of only half or a quarter normal size. Modern beekeeping practices dictate that the hive should be strong, simple and light. Possibly some of the new light plastic materials being used experimentally in hives, combs and frames will help to fulfil these needs.

Figure 10.1 An apiary of hives with double walls, Hertfordshire, England.

Figure 10.2 Apiary of special small hives, from which virgin queens fly to become mated, belonging to Buckfast Abbey, Devon, England.

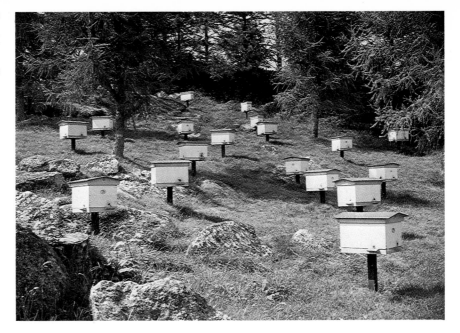

Since the invention and the adoption of the moveable-frame hive, much of the progress has been towards increased mechanisation. As a rule this is more highly developed in the New World than the Old World. This is partly because a greater proportion of bee colonies in the New World are kept by commercial operators and fewer by hobbyists, but it does allow much more efficient use of labour, even when commercial enterprises only are considered, and each beekeeper in parts of North America can be expected to operate about 1000 colonies for honey production or pollination.

Mechanisation is of paramount importance in dealing with the honey crop. For example, an apparatus generating a powerful stream of air forces the bees to abandon boxes containing the honeycombs and so leaves the combs free of bees and ready for the extraction of honey. The wax cappings of the honey cells are removed by power-operated knives or other devices, and honey extractors have now been developed so that boxes of combs can be loaded directly into them. Honey processing has been subjected to much mechanical innovation and efficiency, and honey can be provided in smooth granulated form or as a clear liquid.

The taste and colouration of honey depends much on its floral source, and honeys are often either labelled according to the major crop from which they were collected, for example clover, heather, lime, acacia, orange blossom, or from the country of origin. Because of the increasing use of herbicides to kill weeds before they flower and to promote cleaner agriculture, a jar of honey today is more likely to have been collected from only one or a few floral sources than in the past. This is probably

124

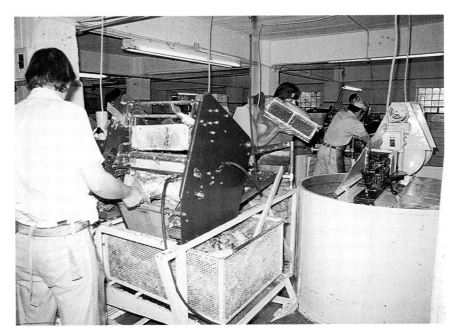

Figure 10.3 Extracting honey by modern methods, Miel Carlota, Mexico.

especially true of the New World, where beekeeping is more intensive and extensive than in the Old World, and where there are usually larger areas of a single floral source.

There is also a marked contrast between the honey yield of colonies in the Old and New Worlds. It is common in the New World to obtain yields of 50 kg per colony; in parts of Western Australia and the western provinces of Canada 100 kg per colony is normal.

In the Old World the yield is much lower, even among the commercial beekeepers, and much of Europe does not produce sufficient honey for its own needs. This is mainly because the concentration of colonies is much greater and the forage available less, so that colony management for honey production can be an intriguing challenge. However, because local honey usually sells at a premium over imported honey, there is less difference in the commercial beekeepers' incomes than might at first be apparent.

Some countries, e.g. Australia, Mexico and Argentina, both produce and export much honey. Others, e.g. the USA, Canada and New Zealand, produce and consume much honey, and countries such as Britain, Germany and Japan consume much more than they produce. In general, a high rate of honey consumption is characteristic of families with a high income, living in affluent societies. This contrasts with the situation in the Middle Ages when the peasant beekeeper produced and consumed his own honey, but was quite unable to afford the then expensive sugar.

Honey consumption per person per year is about 1 kg in Switzerland 125 and the German Federal Republic, about 0.5 kg in the USA, and about 0.25 kg in France, Italy, Japan and the UK. The German Federal Republic is the largest importer with 50 000 tonnes of honey imported per year, followed by the USA, Japan and the UK with 21 000, 18 000 and 17 000 tonnes, respectively. During the past few years, honey consumption in Japan has increased spectacularly.

A recent conference organised by the International Trade Centre and 'Apimondia' forecast a slow increase in the consumption of table honey in most countries, and a rapid increase in a few. This demand will probably be stimulated by the increased interest being shown in natural foods and health products.

To many beekeepers in the Old World and to an increasing number in the New World, the fascination of the bees is of far more importance than the amount of honey produced. Many take enormous pride in their hobby, with an intriguing array of gadgets and personal inventions, and beautifully designed and executed beehives and beehouses, which, if not the most efficient, are certainly for the most part aesthetically pleasing.

Increased ease of transport and communication during the past half century has facilitated the widespread distribution of various strains of *Apis mellifera*. Indeed, commercial beekeeping in some of the northern States of the USA and the western provinces of Canada, where wintering colonies is difficult or uneconomical, depends upon the importation each spring of packages of adult bees reared by specialist beekeepers in the southern USA. Other beekeepers specialise in producing queens for sale; the purity of selected stock may be maintained by artificial insemination of the virgin queens with the semen of drones of known parentage.

Apis mellifera has been introduced to Asia, where it competes with the other three *Apis* species; in Japan, *Apis mellifera* has almost completely replaced the native *Apis cerana* in commercial apiaries. Unfortunately, the immigrant bees have too often carried their diseases with them; but the great strides that have been made in our understanding of honeybee adult and brood diseases during the past few decades now enable most of these to be controlled.

Migratory beekeeping is the moving of colonies from one source of forage to another as it comes into flower. Most of the honey crop of Western Australia, where honeybees were not introduced until 1822, is obtained by moving colonies from forest areas of one species of *Eucalyptus* to another as they come into flower in succession; as the forest is cleared, so the honey yield diminishes. Not only does migratory beekeeping allow colonies to gather from a succession of crops that might otherwise not be available to them at all, but by placing the colonies at the site of a crop, the individual foragers use far less time and energy flying to and fro, and so their productivity per bee can be greatly increased. This is especially so in dull cloudy weather, when bees from colonies some distance from a source of forage often stay at home, while those whose colonies are beside the forage continue to work it.

The concept of migratory beekeeping is not new. There are records of hives being moved to the lower slopes of Mount Hymettus in Attica, Greece, as early as 600 BC, and we have seen that in Ancient Egypt colonies were loaded on rafts which were moved along the River Nile as the flowering of the crops dictated. In 1680 John Evelyn wrote:

> We are told they use this custom still about Holland and Zeland in the season that the Turneps are in flower, and we have known a Bee Master in our own Country that was wont to place his hives in Fields of Buckwheate for this purpose, to his very great advantage.

In parts of Saudi Arabia today, log hives are transported by camel from one elevation to another to take advantage of different times of local flowering.

However, migratory beekeeping today is usually greatly facilitated by the ease with which modern hives may be closed and ventilated for transport, by the large carrying capacity of modern trucks, by good roads, and by mechanical loading devices which allow one man alone to perform the whole operation of loading and unloading a truckload of hives with comparative ease. Although originally developed for honey production, the techniques of migratory beekeeping have become invaluable for pollination services.

Despite more intensive agriculture, which has destroyed many flowering wild plants, increased mechanisation of beekeeping, and the ability of the commercial beekeeper to take advantage of large areas of natural and cultivated flowering crops by migrating to them, has resulted in increased honey production in modern times. About 50 million honeybee colonies are kept by the world's beekeepers, producing about 600 000 tonnes of honey annually. This is insufficient; world demand had increased considerably during recent years.

The contrast between different types of beekeeping in the world today is now greater than it has ever been before; contrasts that are exemplified by the highly efficient beekeeper of North America or Australia, who produces large quantities of high quality, hygenically packed honey, to the honey hunter of Africa, who often destroys the colony he discovers and either eats the honey and brood direct from the comb, or brews the honey into an alcoholic drink, discarding the comb in the process.

The treatment and processing of harvested honey differs much even among countries with modern beekeeping enterprises. Some honey is merely strained before being retailed; other honey is briefly heated, filtered under pressure, and 'seeded' with finely granulated honey to give a uniform soft smooth product.

In most industrialised countries, honey production is unlikely to increase, and may even decline as the areas of agricultural crops diminish. Exceptions may occur when crops such as oil seed rape, that produce abundant nectar, become economically attractive. But in general the increase in world demand for honey can only be satisfied by boosting honey production in developing countries; fortunately there is much potential for improvement.

In contrast, developing countries in Africa and South America can already be counted amongst the largest exporters of beeswax, which is also in short supply. A total of 5000 tonnes of beeswax, about 80–90% of the total available, is imported by seven industrialised countries: the USA, West Germany, the UK, Japan, France, the Netherlands and Switzerland.

Nearly 40% of all beeswax is used by the cosmetics industry. Manufacturers of pharmaceuticals take a further 25–30%, and most of the remainder is used in the production of church candles. The rising standard of living in many countries is resulting in an increasing demand for cosmetics. Beeswax also finds important uses in dentistry casting, lithography, engraving, polishes, confectionery and armaments. Its competitors are paraffin wax, microcrystalline waxes and synthetic waxes, but in many cases the customer shows a marked preference for the natural product. This preference is likely to be maintained in the immediate future.

From time to time special qualities, usually associated with the ability to improve human health, have been attributed not only to honey but to other products of the bee colony, including bee-collected pollen and propolis, bee venom and the brood food ('royal jelly') secreted by the worker bee. As a result, special techniques have been developed to produce these substances commercially.

A novel use of bees, still being developed, is for sampling an area to determine the mineral content of the soil. It is known that the mineral content of plants tends to reflect that of their environment, although different species do so to different extents. Because of this variation between species, it is wise to select plant samples from as wide a spectrum as possible. The pollen collected by a honeybee colony during a single day represents thousands of plants of several species in an area of several square kilometres, so it seemed likely that pollen-collecting bees could be ideal sampling agents. It has now been demonstrated that the mineral content of bee-collected pollen corresponds to that of the soil both in areas of south-western England whose soil has a relatively high mineral content and in areas of eastern England whose soil has a known low metal composition. Thus pollen-collecting bees could be

128

used in determining the agricultural potential of an area, in prospecting for metals and in discovering the presence of an abnormally high mineral content which might be detrimental to human health.

Honey and beeswax production today

Bees for pollination

To make a prairie it takes a clover and one bee.

Emily Dickinson

The use of bees for pollination is already an integral part of much of modern crop production, and is likely to become of increasing importance in the future.

POLLINATION NEEDS

Go to your fields and your gardens, and you shall learn that it is the pleasure
   of the bee to gather honey of the flower,
But it is also the pleasure of the flower to yield its honey to the bee
For to the bee a flower is a fountain of life,
And to the flower a bee is a messenger of love,
And to both, bee and flower, the giving and the receiving of pleasure is a
   need and an ecstasy.

Kahlil Gibran, *The Prophet*

Some plants are 'self-fertile' and can produce viable seed when their stigmas are 'self-pollinated' with pollen from the anthers of the same plant. The parts of some self-fertile flowers are so arranged that pollen automatically falls from a flower's anthers on its own stigmas (e.g. garden pea, peanut, chickpea, flax and tobacco), although their structure indicates that in the evolutionary past they were once insect-pollinated. Usually, however, such auto-pollination is prevented or limited and pollen has to be transferred by an external agent. Other plants are 'self-sterile' and need to be 'cross-pollinated' with pollen from the anthers of another plant; an external agent is always necessary to transfer the pollen. Cross-pollination may also give better yields from plants that are self-fertile.

Wind and insects are the main pollinating agents of commercial crops. Wind is responsible for pollinating cereals and other grasses, nut trees and a few other crops, whose pollen is light and dry and easily carried by air currents. Most other commercial crops which have heavy sticky pollen benefit to some extent from insect pollination. Plants traditionally supposed to be wind-pollinated may benefit from insect pollination; thus, we now know that the oil palm is primarily insect-pollinated and not wind-pollinated, as was previously supposed. It is estimated that

129

about one third of the food produced in the USA is dependent directly or indirectly upon insect-pollinated plants.

A standard method of determining whether a crop benefits from insect pollination is to enclose plants in insect-proof cages and to compare the fruit or seed produced in cages where honeybees are present with that in cages where they are absent. When cages are not available, individual flowers or flower heads may be bagged so that pollinating insects are excluded; it is important that some of these bagged flowers are hand-pollinated to find the maximum set possible under these conditions. Both methods have disadvantages; cages, even large ones, by altering the microclimate, may influence plant growth and response to pollination; bagging individual flowers may greatly influence the microclimate of the flower itself and the auto-pollination process. However, the results of such research have been of great value to the grower.

Crops differ in their response to insect pollination. Some (e.g. blackberry, gooseberry, raspberry, field bean, okra, opium poppy and safflower) give only a moderately increased yield when pollinated by insects; others (e.g. blueberry, mustard, rape, turnip, cashew, guava, mango and peach) give a greatly increased yield, and yet others (including clovers, runner bean and various varieties of apple, pear and plum) yield little or no fruit or seed unless insect-pollinated.

However, pollination by insects sometimes has advantages in addition to greater seed or fruit yield. For example, increased pollination can induce a greater proportion of early flowers to set seed, and so gives an earlier and more uniform crop with less loss at harvest. Pollination can also influence the quality as well as the quantity of the crop; when pollination is inadequate, small lopsided or otherwise misshapen and inferior fruits may be formed.

Many kinds of insects visit the flowers of commercial crops. Although a few kinds eat the floral parts, many transfer at least some pollen grains and so may help in pollination. However, relatively few are consistently good pollinators. The most efficient pollinators are those that carry plenty of pollen on their bodies, brush against the stigmas of flowers transferring the pollen, visit several flowers of the same species in succession, and move frequently from flower to flower and, for crops needing cross-pollination, from plant to plant. Because of their behaviour, small size and smooth body surfaces many insects are poor pollinators. Bees, whose bodies are covered with branched hairs, are the most important. Various hairy flies carry as much pollen as bees, but they do not forage as consistently. Pollen and nectar provide bees with their sole source of protein and carbohydrate, and whereas most insects forage only to satisfy their immediate needs, bees forage consistently to collect sufficient food for their young and to add to their stores.

130   To find the pollinating efficiency of a particular type of insect,

individual flowers or clusters of flowers should be bagged while still in the bud stage, and when the flowers have opened, the bags are removed until the flowers are visited by the insect; they are then bagged again and the proportion of visited flowers that produce seed determined.

AVAILABILITY OF POLLINATING INSECTS

I thought of the last honey by the water
That no hive can find.

Austin Clarke, 'The Lost Heifer'

The basic concept of insect pollination of flowers was discovered over 200 years ago, but little economic importance was attached to it until well into this century, probably because a wealth of wild pollinators (bees, flies and other insects) ensured that pollination was adequate and unlikely to be the factor limiting fruit or seed set. Even in these circumstances, as in the Tropics today, bees were of primary importance because of their behaviour and greater efficiency at transporting pollen. Indeed, probably at first man encouraged wild bees as he cleared the primeval forests, allowing light to penetrate and plant species to multiply. Studies in northwestern Canada have shown that the population of wild bees is greatest soon after the forest has been cleared, when there are many small fields and much waste ground.

The situation has now changed, and during the past few decades the populations of wild bees and other insects have become inadequate to pollinate crops in many parts of the world.

Some factors may actually decrease the number of wild pollinators. Clean and intensive cultivation of the land, including the destruction of hedgerows, banks and rough verges, regular mowing of roadside verges and around field crops, and use of selective herbicides has reduced available nesting and hibernating sites, and also lessened the number of flowering plants that help to provide beneficial insects with food.

Most insects that forage on plants damage them and diminish their capacity to propagate themselves; the greater the numbers of the pest insect the less is the likelihood that the host plant will reproduce. In contrast, a pollinating insect encourages reproduction of its host plant, and so tends to increase the plant population and the amount of nectar and pollen available for its own future generations. However, with fewer pollinators, the propagation of wild flowers will decline, together with the population of pollinators they can support, increasing the difficulties for pollinators to return to their original populations.

The damage done to wild pollinators by insecticide application is largely unknown, but this is probably a contributory factor – and too often the most important one – in reducing their numbers. Certainly pesticides are often responsible for honeybee poisoning. Most poison- 131 ing occurs while bees are foraging and the insecticide damage to honeybee colonies differs according to many factors, including its toxicity, its method and time of day of application, the number of applications, the proportion of foragers visiting the crop being treated, the species of crop concerned and its floral structure, the foraging behaviour of bees on the crop, and the 'drift' of insecticide to other sources of forage.

A few examples of poisoning must suffice. Application of insecticide to cotton has been foremost in causing honeybee losses in the USA, and its use in some of the cotton-growing areas of Tanzania and Kenya has made beekeeping impossible. Use of insecticide in bean-growing areas of northern Tanzania has destroyed beekeeping in the immediate vicinity. The blanket aerial application of pesticide, as currently practised in parts of Arabia, kills many honeybees, and probably other beneficial insects as well.

In many circumstances, pesticide application is unnecessary and is applied at far below the economic threshold of pest incidence. For example, the recorded incidents of honeybee poisoning with insecticide applied to oil seed rape in England have increased with the amount of rape grown. However, research has shown that most levels of pest infestation found in oil seed rape in England probably do not justify control measures, especially since oil seed rape plants have considerable powers of compensatory growth; so much insecticide has been applied needlessly.

The misapplication of micro-encapsulated insecticides constitutes a new hazard to beekeeping in the USA. The capsules, which are about the same size as pollen grains, become incorporated into the pollen loads of foraging bees and stored in the hive, where the slow release of the insecticide can destroy both adult bees and brood.

Strong evidence that insecticides diminish the numbers of wild pollinators is difficult to obtain. One of the best examples is from New Brunswick, Canada. Aerial application of the organophosorus insecticide fenitrothrion to control spruce budworm in the forests caused a marked depression in populations of wild bees shortly afterwards, and diminished yields of blueberry fruits. Forest plants flowering during this period also showed diminished seed and fruit production. Application of fenitrothrion in the vicinity of the blueberry fields ceased in 1976 and an insecticide with low toxicity to bees was substituted. The bee population in the affected areas now appears to be increasing.

It is to be hoped that the poisoning of bees and other beneficial insects will diminish as their value becomes more widely appreciated and the minimum use of insecticides is integrated with a maximum use of biological and cultural control. The difficulty will probably not be fully resolved until an insecticide is developed which selectively favours bees and other beneficial insects.

The decrease in numbers of wild pollinating insects tends to be associated with an increased need for pollination. In many parts of the Tropics each farmer tends to cultivate small plots, often of a few rows only, of several different food crops. In contrast, in temperate countries there have been changes in agricultural practice from small fields to large fields, and from small orchards, of many types of fruit, near the farmhouse to large orchards of only one or two varieties. This increase in crop size has increased pollination needs while a crop is flowering, so that even though the number of wild insect pollinators present in an area was able to cope in the past, it is too small to be able to do so now. The tendency to concentrate particular crops in certain areas intensifies the situation.

Large areas of a single flowering crop can provide ample nectar and pollen. Indeed, changes in crop fashion may have pronounced effects on the amount of forage available. The amount of oil seed rape grown in southern England has increased greatly during the past decade. Bee-keepers often find it worthwhile to move their honeybee colonies to the rape crops for the honey produced; other beneficial insects, including syrphids and bumblebees, also visit rape flowers for nectar and pollen. Indeed, winter- and spring-sown rape occurring in the same locality provides a source of forage to bumblebees from colony initiation to the climax of colony development and the production of sexual forms. Although, in the short term, rape crops may attract bumblebees from other crops that need pollination (e.g. clover, field bean, runner bean, tree fruit), in the long term, especially where bumblebee populations are limited by the amount of forage available, the large areas of rape now grown in England will encourage them and so be of general benefit.

However, although a major crop can provide abundant forage for a short time, when it is not in flower there may be too few other flowering plants in the vicinity to support the population of pollinating insects that are needed and to provide food for honeybee colonies to overwinter. A continuous sequence of nectar and pollen plants is of prime importance for successful beekeeping. Therefore, large scale monoculture, which is necessary for the economic production of mechanically cultivated and harvested crops, results in an increased need for pollinating insects, but can reduce the populations of native pollinators and the profitability of beekeeping.

While growers should wish to ensure that there are sufficient wild flowers in their locality to encourage wild pollinators, it is unrealistic to expect them to provide land that could otherwise grow crops for this purpose.

However, if possible, use should be made of suitable spare land including, of course, that bordering roads and railways. Indeed, compared to other reservoirs of wild flower species, the large verges of

133

motorways and trunk roads often have the advantage that they form a continuous habitat, extending over large areas of the countryside, that is inaccessible to the general public. The seed mixture planted on motorway verges could possibly be modified to contain flowering perennials of value to beneficial insects. Ideally, species chosen for planting should flower at times when nearby crops needing pollination are not flowering. Early- and late-flowering species would be especially valuable. But even if flowering of these species did partly coincide with that of some crops needing pollination, and so would compete with them temporarily, this disadvantage would be more than offset by the forage they provide through the rest of the season, including dearth periods when agricultural crops are not in flower.

The US Department of Agriculture have recently instigated a research programme to find the most suitable nectar and pollen plants for reclaiming disturbed areas.

PROVIDING POLLINATING INSECTS

How I love the hum of the drowsy bee,
And the whir of the insect wings.

Lorma Leigh, 'Amaranthe'

Fortunately, the deficit in pollinating insects can usually be overcome. For an insect to be used efficiently as a pollinator, it should be easily handled and available in large numbers. Apart from bees, only blowflies have so far filled these criteria because commercial producers of blowfly maggots for fishbait could also supply pupae. Unlike bees, blowflies do not have a home base or nest, so do not forage in a restricted area, but they are useful for pollinating open or shallow flowers with easily accessible nectaries, in cages or under glass, and may be as effective as bees. Their total contribution to crop pollination is relatively insignificant when compared to the honeybee.

The bumblebee is an efficient pollinator of many crops, and is especially valuable in pollinating flowers with deep narrow corollae from which only insects with long tongues can obtain nectar, and in pollinating flowers that need visits of large insects to transfer pollen.

Solitary bees and honeybees find difficulty in obtaining nectar from red clover because the distance from the tip of the corolla to the nectar often exceeds the reach of the bee's tongue; this difficulty is intensified with tetraploid red clover which has a longer corolla tube. Bumblebees are important pollinators of red clover, and in northern Europe efforts are made to grow red clover for seed in areas where bumblebees are usually abundant. However, although bumblebees are valuable pollinators, their populations are unpredictable and may fluctuate greatly.

Figure 10.4
Bumblebee, *Bombus pascuolum* foraging on red clover *(Trifolium repens)*. Its long tongue is especially adapted to reach the nectar at the bases of long narrow flowers.

Many attempts have been made to increase the bumblebee populations where they are specifically needed, either by providing artificial nest-sites for queens in spring, or by inducing queens to nest in especially prepared domiciles in the laboratory which can later be taken to crops needing pollination. Promising results have recently been obtained by both these methods, but they are still unreliable and many colonies that are initiated in captivity fail to mature. Basically, this is because the factors governing bumblebee ovary development, nest searching and colony initiation are not fully understood. Hence, although the prospect of providing bumblebee colonies for pollination on a commercial scale has improved during the last few years, the present methods are too laborious to be economically justifiable.

In contrast, two species of solitary bee are already used commercially for alfalfa pollination in North America. One, the alkali bee, *Nomia melanderi*, nests in soil that is sub-irrigated, and specialised processes are necessary to create new sites. The other, the leaf cutter, *Megachile rotundata* (p. 10), which occupies a variety of nest-sites including beetle burrows, nail holes, hollow stems and fissures in logs, also readily occupies artificial nest-sites, and techniques have been developed to induce it to nest and multiply in artificial domiciles that are put beside alfalfa crops needing pollination. Careful management practices are sometimes necessary to protect these bees from parasites, disease and predators.

Encouraged by the exploitation of these two species of solitary bee, a search for other suitable bees to act as crop pollinators is being made among the many thousands of wild species. A solitary bee that has been encouraged to nest in bamboo and hollow reeds in fruit orchards in

135

Figure 10.5 Female alkali bee *(Nomia melanderi)* at the entrance to her nest (photo by W. P. Nye).

Figure 10.6 Shelter containing nests of the leaf-cutter bee *(Megachile rotundata)* at edge of an alfalfa field.

Japan has now been introduced into North America. No doubt many solitary-bee species will be able to live in artificial nests, but for commercial use a species must be gregarious, rapidly increase its population in man-made nests, visit the flowers of a commercial crop in preference to those of other crops, have a peak of activity coinciding with that of the flowering crop, be easily manipulated and managed, and not be subject to uncontrollable parasites and disease. It is well known that many

136 species of solitary bee visit alfalfa in different parts of the world,

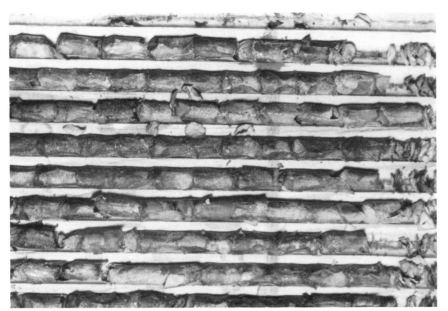

Figure 10.7 Tunnels of the shelter opened to show leaf-cutter bee *(Megachile rotundata)* nests built inside (photo by W. P. Nye).

although most are too scarce to be of much value. For example, in Hungary a recent survey recorded 140 wild bee species in alfalfa fields, 30 of them appearing regularly. Possibly, if such species were introduced to different parts of the world, they would occupy ecological niches not fully exploited by native species, and some might fulfil the above criteria.

The use of solitary bees for pollinating particular crops, both temperate and tropical, will surely increase. Some countries have imported the leaf-cutter bee, *Megachile rotundata*, from North America, and when other suitable species are found it is likely that they will be introduced elsewhere. Solitary bees that forage only on the crop concerned, even in the presence of competition, and whose flight activity coincides with that of the crop, are likely to be less harmed by monoculture than bees with more catholic tastes, although they are most vulnerable if the crop is treated with insecticide.

Amongst other wild bees deserving of study are the social stingless bees of Central and South America, Africa and Asia. Little is known of their foraging behaviour and their potential use as pollinators of commercial crops is unexplored. It is to be hoped that the situation will soon be rectified. Meanwhile, it is important to conserve them and ensure that they have adequate nesting sites.

USING HONEYBEES

> She pleases God, she pleases man,
> She does the work that no man can.
>
> Anonymous

The present situation However, the honeybee will probably remain our most important pollinating insect. Its main advantages are that during its life, and even during a single day, a honeybee visits many flowers and distributes abundant pollen; it is less influenced by low temperatures and low light intensity than solitary bees and has more catholic tastes, visiting and pollinating a large proportion of crop species; its biology is well known as a result of years of accumulated experience and study, and, because bees have long been kept for honey production, techniques for managing colonies already exist; because it lives in large colonies it can readily be introduced in large numbers as and where required, even to areas such as irrigated crops in desert regions where few other pollinating insects exist.

Because there are insufficient wild pollinators, and because experiments have demonstrated the greater yield of many crops when adequately pollinated, the demand for honeybee colonies for pollination has greatly increased, particularly during the past few years. Indeed, the value of the honeybee as a pollinator now far exceeds its value as a producer of honey and wax, and it is likely that the commercial use of honeybees for pollination will continue to expand.

In countries where land is used intensively, honey crops, and the profitability of keeping bees for honey production, have sometimes decreased in recent years, but an increased demand for honeybee colonies for pollination will probably provide an economic incentive for keeping bees. It is essential that beekeeping should continue to provide bees for pollination.

Figure 10.8 Modern hives in an orchard near Esfahan, Iran.

It is important that the true value of the pollinating activities of the honeybee are recognised and that the beekeeper is paid an adequate wage for hire of his colonies. At present, the type of payment made for hire of honeybee colonies for pollination tends to reflect the political nature of the society concerned. But, in general, the amount the grower is prepared to pay depends upon the extent to which he thinks his net profits will be increased. The amount the beekeeper demands will partly be determined by transport costs and the extent to which his potential honey crop will be diminished, because the honeybee population needed for adequate seed or fruit set may be much greater than the area will support for profitable honey production.

The number of honeybee colonies needed to pollinate a crop will depend on the crop's pollination needs, its size, the density of its flowers, the amount of nectar and pollen available, the attractiveness of the flowers to bees, bees' behaviour on the crop and their ability to pollinate it, the colonies' foraging populations, and the number of wild pollinating insects already present. Whereas a flower of some species (e.g. alfalfa) needs to receive only one visit before it sets seed, others (e.g. melon) need several bee visits each before sufficient seeds are set to produce a marketable product. Often it is only necessary for a proportion of the available flowers to set to provide a commercial crop or before the carrying capacity of the plant is reached. Because of these and other variables, the grower must determine for himself the effect on seed or fruit set of progressively increasing the number of colonies present. If he finds that pollinating a sample of flowers by hand increases their set, then insect pollination is inadequate and more honeybee colonies are needed.

Whereas nearly every visit by suitable pollinating insects to flowers that can be self-pollinated could lead to fertilisation, only a small proportion of such visits to female flowers needing cross-pollination could be expected to do so. This is one reason why a large population of honeybees is needed to pollinate fruit flowers that set fruit only when they are cross-pollinated. When foraging in fruit orchards of standard trees, a bee visits only about two trees per foraging trip and the moves it makes between trees are usually between adjacent ones. As a result, trees next to a polleniser variety may be better pollinated than trees further away. Indeed, the sides of main variety trees facing polleniser trees may have a greater fruit set, more seeds per fruit, and more carpels with seeds per fruit than the far sides.

In an attempt to compensate for lack of adequate set, and smooth out fluctuations in yield, various devices for artificially dispensing pollen in fruit orchards have been tried. But these have been abandoned as it has become apparent that there are no satisfactory substitutes for consistent bee visits to crops as new flowers open.

139

Although cross-pollination is more difficult to achieve than self-pollination, it is associated with plant vigour and species survival, and most flowering plants have evolved various devices to encourage it. These include the separation of male and female flowers on different plants, the maturing of the male and female parts of hermaphrodite flowers at different times, and self-incompatibility.

Exploitation of hybrid vigour to obtain greater yields of agricultural crops is increasing. Parental cultivars are selected and crossed to produce 'hybrid' seed that gives uniform and high quality offspring when grown commercially. In the next season, hybrid seed for distribution to growers is again produced from these same two chosen parental cultivars, thus ensuring that the same hybrid line is maintained. Because hybrid seed production depends on insects carrying pollen from 'male' to 'female' plants, it is creating a special demand for cross-pollination.

The relatively small foraging areas of individual bees are advantageous when attempts are made to grow uncontaminated seed, because they help to prevent undesirable cross-pollination. When compatible cultivars are in adjacent plots, contamination with foreign pollen is intensive where they adjoin and then rapidly diminishes as the distance separating them increases. However, a small amount (1 or 2%) of contamination persists far from the undesirable pollen source. This is because pollen that is transferred between bees as they brush against each other within the hive between foraging trips can cause cross-pollination over long distances, although the individual bees remain constant to a small area. The only completely safe way of isolating plants for seed is to grow and pollinate them in insect-proof cages. Honeybees, bumblebees, solitary bees and blowflies can be used to pollinate in such enclosures; they can also be used to pollinate food crops and ornamental flowers grown under glass or in polythene tunnels in the cool seasons. This is another aspect of pollination that is likely to increase.

If growers acted upon the full implications of findings from pollination research, there would be too few colonies to cope with their demands. This is already true for some crops and in some countries. Therefore it is essential that colonies hired for pollination should do the task as efficiently as possible. A number of practices help to ensure that this is so.

First, the colonies should be taken to the crop needing pollination. Even when colonies are only a short distance away from a crop, the proportion of foragers that visit it can be greatly diminished, particularly during poor foraging weather. Whenever possible, the colonies should be distributed throughout the crop; for example, in fruit orchards small equidistant groups of five colonies each in the centre of a 2 ha area ensure an even distribution of the bees.

The concentration of colonies required for pollination may well over-exploit the floral resources, but even when adequate forage from a single species is available near to a honeybee colony, a proportion of the foraging force will still forage on diverse species further afield. This behaviour may be beneficial to the colony because of the overall nutritional value of a range of pollen from different species. However, the proportion not visiting the crop can be greatly reduced by delaying the taking of colonies to the crop until it has started to flower; this discourages many of the foragers from becoming conditioned to visiting other flower species which they do not readily forsake.

On most crops, pollen gatherers are more efficient pollinators than nectar gatherers because they are more likely to carry a greater amount of pollen on their bodies and transfer pollen to the stigmas. It has been demonstrated that pollen collection may be encouraged by ensuring that the colonies have plenty of brood, by arranging for foragers to be directed to the vicinity of the brood on their return from the field, by feeding colonies with sugar syrup, and by not allowing colonies moved to a new site to fly until the time of day when pollen is available from the crop needing pollination.

One way to increase crop visitation is to breed honeybee colonies with preferences for particular crops; sufficient work has been done to show that this is possible. Some 20 years ago selection began on honeybee strains that showed a preference for alfalfa pollen; however, the early promise has not been maintained, and it has not proved to be a commercial success. Perhaps it will prove more profitable to attempt to select strains with an enhanced tendency to collect pollen. There seems to be no reason why the less aggressive strains of honeybee should not be selected for pollination work. Docility need not be associated with loss of pollinating efficiency and could be a major factor in encouraging growers to use honeybee colonies.

Conversely, plants could be bred for increased attractiveness to bees. For example, it is known that honeybees can discriminate between different alfalfa clones by their different floral odours, and some are preferred to others. It may be possible to select for these attractive volatile components, and enhance their effect by conditioning bees to them. However, we still have much to learn about the factors that make one plant more attractive than others to insect visitors.

Research is needed to produce better estimates than we have at present of the bee populations needed to pollinate specific crops. Calculations will need to be based on the working rate per bee, the time available for pollination, the number of flowers present, the percentage of flowers to be pollinated, and the pollinating efficiency per bee visit. The last-mentioned piece of information will be the most difficult to obtain and will occupy most time; it will sometimes need to include studies

141

on the readiness with which bees transfer pollen between different varieties.

Further studies on the organisation of the honeybee colony will perhaps provide new information that is relevant to foraging and help us to produce colonies that are more effective pollinating units. For example, we need more information on the relative foraging efficiency of colonies of different sizes, and with different proportions of brood to adults, before we can judge whether it is worth providing colonies with sugar syrup and pollen substitute to stimulate growth in early spring or to maintain colony strength during dearth periods. In this connection we need to find a cheap pollen substitute whose nutritional value equals or surpasses that of pollen. If we could identify and synthesise the attractant in pollen, it could be added to pollen substitutes to make them more acceptable to bees, and perhaps be applied to crops to attract bees to them.

Where honeybee colonies are hired to pollinate agricultural and horticultural crops, much pollination by honeybees occurs incidentally and not only helps increase commercial food production but also enables many of our wild plants, including soil-enriching and soil-holding species, to reproduce. The seed or fruit produced by herbaceous plants, shrubs and trees in turn support many wild animals. In addition very many flowers and fruits are aesthetically pleasing to man; indeed many are cultivated for no other purpose:

> 'The flowers that bloom unknown for a thousand years only exist when at least one flower blossoms under a perceptive eye. For that flower the pollen was launched spring after spring, the nectar gathered, the seed rounded' (Mary Webb).

Hence the conservation value of honeybees is enormous, although immeasurable.

Because the amount of honey produced is still the prime factor in determining whether keeping honeybee colonies is economically profitable, efforts should be made to favour planting trees and shrubs from which honeybees are known to obtain large amounts of nectar and pollen. In arid areas, trees and bushes planted to provide recreational facilities should also be selected to provide good bee forage; many acacias and mesquites are excellent nectar producers and thrive under dry conditions. As Keats put it:

> To set budding more
> And still more flowers for the bees,
> Until they think warm days will never cease,
> For summer has o'er brimmed their clammy cells.

Beekeeping for wax or honey will inevitably help pollination. But beekeeping must no longer be considered in the restricted roles of honey and wax production. It is important that beekeeping for pollination should be encouraged whatever the honey and wax crops may be. Indeed, it is likely that honey may sometimes become a by-product of beekeeping for pollination as, in many parts of the world, wax has now become a by-product of honey production.

Encouraging beekeeping in developing countries

> Mine be a cot beside the hill;
> A bee-hive's hum shall soothe my ear.
>
> S. Rogers, 'A Wish'

The resources of the Earth are limited and must not be allowed to go to waste. There are two most important reasons for encouraging beekeeping in developing countries, both of which should result in an improvement of the world's food supply. The first is for an increase in the production of honey and wax and other products of the hive; the second is for an increase in the yield of many tropical crops by increased pollination. Variation in the efficiency and sophistication of beekeeping throughout the world is as great, or greater, as that in most other branches of agriculture.

Some primitive methods of beekeeping may yield only 1–2 kg of honey per colony compared with up to 100 kg of honey per colony in those parts of the world where the most intensive methods of management are employed. Indeed, beekeeping is a branch of agriculture that is more capable than most of rapid overall improvement, and world demand and increasing prices make for an almost certain market for the honey and wax produced.

The encouragement of beekeeping in developing countries has the additional advantage that it is relatively inexpensive compared with other agricultural activities, so that bees can be kept by the rural poor. Little land (which can be of poor quality) is required to provide the site for the hives, equipment can be inexpensive, and an individual can decide the extent to which he is willing to commit himself to a beekeeping enterprise. Beekeeping can start as a spare-time occupation using simple methods and cheap hives and progressively graduate to a part-time or full-time occupation, using better equipment and more profitable methods, as money becomes available. Although the prime object may be to establish beekeeping at the family or subsistence level, where most, if not all, of the honey is consumed by its producer, there is no reason why it should not develop into a commercial enterprise later.

Most of the unexploited honey-producing regions are in the Tropics and sub-Tropics, and the nectar and pollen supplies available are going to waste. For example, it is estimated that in India the number of colonies of *Apis cerana* kept by beekeepers will need to increase from

143

600 000 to 50 million to exploit fully the nectar sources and pollinate the crops. Indonesia has the potential to produce 80 000 tonnes of honey a year, mostly from its forest areas. Kenya, with vast potential for honey production, still imports from Europe, New Zealand and Australia.

By selecting trees for afforestation programmes that provide nectar and pollen, an additional bonus can be given to honey and wax production. This is especially true of eucalyptus forests. In Java, attempts are being made to introduce beekeeping to people living near forests, and by raising their living standards help to implement forest protection.

However, before any attempt is made to encourage beekeeping in a particular area, it is essential to determine whether the area concerned can profitably support it, otherwise much effort can be wasted. Ideally, this should be done in two ways. First, the local flora should be examined to obtain an indication of the sources and amount of nectar and pollen likely to be available at different times of the year; in India, for example, a detailed picture of the best areas and times of year for honey production is being obtained by this method. Second, it is advisable to examine the food stores in any colonies – wild or in hives – that exist in the area, to determine the floral sources which they have been working; the presence of colonies in the area itself indicates that enough food is available for them to survive.

If it then seems that the area is promising, a small test apiary of modern hives should be established and maintained for at least 2 years to determine what the honey production potential is likely to be and to

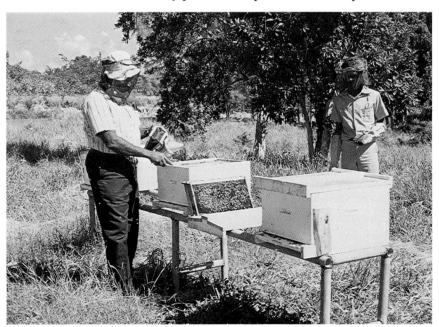

Figure 10.9 One of a series of government demonstration apiaries established in Jamaica.

give time for any management problems peculiar to the area to become apparent. By taking regular samples of newly collected nectar and pollen, and collating them with gain or loss in weight of hives, further information on the relative importance of the various flower species as producers of nectar and pollen can be obtained. This will enable bee-keepers to locate their colonies in the most favourable sites. These 'test' or demonstration apiaries are invaluable as teaching aids.

If the honey yield is satisfactory and there are no serious obstacles to beekeeping, efforts can be made to encourage it. There is little need for any immediate research, and any problem that arises on beekeeping techniques and equipment can probably be solved by the application of knowledge and principles already available. However, much more information will need to be acquired before beekeeping and honey production can be fully exploited.

The type of beekeeping attempted and the type of equipment used will depend on local circumstances, on whether beekeeping in the area is primarily for honey or for wax, and on the amount of financial aid available.

Many parts of the world, especially those covered largely by forest and jungle, are inaccessible by road and there is great difficulty in transporting honey crops. In such areas, where primitive beekeeping or honey hunting is practised, the honey is squeezed out of the comb and is usually consumed locally, often as honey beer in Africa, and comb containing pollen and brood is eaten. Much of the wax is discarded by the hunters. Because wax is easier to transport than honey, preservation of old comb should be encouraged, and central pick-up locations arranged where possible.

Local beekeepers and honey hunters usually know little about the biology of the honeybee colony, and should be taught that to leave some combs with brood and honey will enable the colony to survive and produce more harvests.

In other places, which are reasonably accessible by road, modern bee-hives and frames to hold the combs may be too expensive for the inhabitants; for this reason hives made of hollow logs, bark, clay, basketwork or crude wooden planks are in common use. In such circumstances hives that are cheaper, if less convenient, than the best modern ones are sometimes used; but they should be so constructed that modern hives can easily be introduced later on. For example in Kenya and Tanzania, a transitional type of 'long hive' has been introduced. Basically, they are long wooden boxes, with a row of top bars from which the combs are suspended. The combs can be inspected before harvest; those with honey can be cut off and those with brood and pollen left intact. As a result, the honey is of a better quality than from primitive hives, although its extraction is more difficult than from combs

Figure 10.10
Rectangular hives with
fixed combs, near
Olympia, Greece.

of a modern hive. Although the combs of transitional hives cannot be
returned after the honey is extracted, this need not be a disadvantage
where a market for wax is established.

The top bars of these long transitional hives should be the same width
as those of the wooden frames of the Langstroth hive, so that if and
when the beekeeper wishes to change to modern hives, he can use his
existing combs and bees to stock them. Hives that are especially
designed for particular purposes, such as for transport on camels or
donkeys, should also, if possible, incorporate combs of standard size.
When use of bark hives is unavoidable, the beekeepers should be
encouraged to produce as many as possible from a single tree, and to
choose trees of little value for other purposes.

If the economic and sociological conditions of a country are favourable, modern beekeeping methods should be implemented as soon as
possible. Such circumstances are to be found in countries such as Saudi
Arabia and the Sultanate of Oman, where increasing prosperity and
government help encourage beekeepers using traditional hives, of date
palm and acacia logs, wooden barrels and clay cylinders, to change to
modern hives, with an average of three or more times the yield of honey
per colony. The Langstroth hive, whose comb size is the most commonly used throughout the world, should be chosen. Increased planting
of agricultural, horticultural and amenity crops in many areas of the
Middle East will also increase the beekeeping potential. Countries with
both relatively cheap motor fuel, good roads and a succession of nectar
crops in different parts of the country, have the added advantage that

146

Figure 10.11 Different types of transitional hive under test in Kenya.

migratory beekeeping is economically viable, and colonies may be transported to exploit crops in different regions.

It must always be borne in mind that commercial beekeeping as practised today was largely developed in temperate zones, and it is to be expected that modifications in management will be necessary for successful beekeeping in the Tropics or arid zones. Furthermore, the strains of bee used for beekeeping in temperate zones may have behavioural characteristics that are unsuitable to warmer climates.

No attempt should be made to import bees from abroad until the local strains have been thoroughly evaluated and found wanting, and even then possible importation must be given very serious consideration. It is likely that the local strain will have adapted to the local flora, climate and enemies over many centuries, and any change would probably be a retrograde step. Indeed, the local strain will probably play an important role in any breeding programme that is eventually embarked upon. In addition, there is a danger of importing bee diseases new to the area, or undesirable characteristics that are genetically dominant. The recent spread of a parasitic mite, *Varroa jacobsoni*, with honeybee colonies imported into North Africa, South America and central Europe, and the introduction of an aggressive strain of bee in South America, provide ample warning of the dangers.

Honey hunting may have been responsible for selecting the particularly aggressive strains of honeybee found in parts of Africa; the hunters must have tended to destroy the more docile colonies and left the aggressive strains to multiply. Hopefully, it may be possible to conserve some of the more desirable characteristics of the aggressive bees that were inadvertently introduced from Africa to Brazil. Paradoxically, in

147

southern Oman, where until very recently there was no beekeeping, and certain individuals were esteemed for their skill as honey hunters, the local bee is quite docile!

Progress in beekeeping should not be confined to the two species, *Apis mellifera* and *Apis cerana*, that can be kept in hives. The bees of an *Apis florea* colony do not readily sting, so the honey crop, although often small, can be taken without discomfort. In the interior of northern Oman and parts of southern India, where traditional ways of farming *Apis florea* colonies have been developed, attempts are being made to increase their efficiency. Despite the small amount of honey produced per colony, it is greatly prized. Although the colonies of *Apis dorsata* are fierce, they provide the hunter with a much greater harvest of honey and wax. Indeed, most of the honey eaten in India and Indonesia comes from colonies of this species. Ways of harvesting the honey from *Apis dorsata* colonies without destroying them are being studied in India.

The concept of pollination, and the pollinating value of the bee, are not widely appreciated in primitive societies, and even today some of their beekeepers think of the bee as an enemy of flowers, because once the bee has pollinated the flowers the petals soon fall – mistaken proof of the bee's destructive powers!

Whereas, in countries with advanced and highly mechanised agriculture, the use of bees for pollination has greatly increased during the last 50 years, relatively little attention has been paid to the pollination of tropical crops. This is partly because other factors such as inadequate soil water and poor soil fertility have limited production, and such pollination as does occur is sufficient to provide for the plants' bearing capacity. But with the use of improved cultivars and culture methods and irrigation, pollination may well become the limiting factor, leading to increased demand for pollinating insects.

There are indications that amongst those crops that benefit from insect pollination are the following: avocado, cashew, mango, passion fruit, many citrus varieties, pimento, coffee, cotton, cucurbits, cucumber, melon, sunflower and safflower. The pollination requirements of others, including many types of bean and other legumes grown in the Tropics, are unknown. More information is urgently needed by growers, who can take direct and immediate action without the need for complex equipment or large scale investment, and reap an almost immediate reward. Such information as we do possess has often been obtained in response to a specific problem or an obvious lack of pollination. Detailed studies must be instigated before problems become critical.

Because of different climatic conditions and different insect pollinators it is most unwise to apply findings from temperate countries to tropical ones or from one hot country to another. For example, pollen

tube growth is probably faster in the Tropics, but the tendency for
unpollinated flowers to survive longer than pollinated ones is probably
less pronounced than in temperate regions. Perhaps, while the pollen is
being transported by insects, it becomes desiccated and non-viable
more quickly in hot than in temperate countries.

Fortunately, practices tending to diminish wild pollinator populations
are in general less severe at present in much of the Tropics than in temperate countries, and large areas of vacant bushland, and scattered
holdings, provide ample nest-sites for wild pollinators, including the
wild honeybees.

Many countries in the Tropics and semi-Tropics still have small
plantations of a variety of crops that flower at different times growing in
close proximity. Flowering of a crop is prolonged and less intensive than
in temperate regions. Where growing conditions are favourable,
farmers may take two or three harvests from the same plots during a
year, and at any one time the same crop species may occur in a sequence
of growth stages. Many fruit trees also flower and fruit throughout the
year, although more abundantly at certain periods. Therefore, forage
for bees is often present at all times, and with prolonged crop flowering
fewer pollinators are needed than for crops of equivalent size in a
temperate climate.

However, as fields become larger and agricultural practices more
mechanised in tropical countries, flowering will be more concentrated
and larger pollinator populations will be needed for shorter periods. In
these circumstances the relative value of the honeybee will become
greater, and eventually honeybee colonies managed by beekeepers will
be the major pollinators; this is already happening in some locations
with some crops. So any attempt that a country makes to encourage beekeeping will benefit the pollination of agricultural and horticultural
crops, and result in increased food production. Efforts to expand beekeeping need not, therefore, be justified entirely by the resulting
increase in honey and wax production.

We are on the threshold of a phase of beekeeping development and
expansion that can be even greater than that following the introduction
of the removeable-frame hive over a century ago; the results could be of
incalculable benefit to mankind. In many parts of the Earth the crop is
present in the flowers; it is waiting to be harvested.

The way forward

How doth the little busy bee
Improve each shining hour,
And gather honey all the day
From every opening flower!   Isaac Watts, 'Against Idleness and Mischief'   149

The present situation   Until the present time, progress has been confined to adapting bees' behaviour to provide honey, wax and, more recently, pollination services for man. Efforts have also been made to discourage undesirable activities, notable among which is swarming, and to breed from colonies with desirable attributes, especially increased honey production.

Much of the activity of the members of a honeybee colony is co-ordinated by chemical messages ('pheromones'). Research is now being undertaken to determine the nature of these behaviour-controlling chemicals and their role in colony organisation and cohesion. By providing appropriate behavioural and chemical stimuli, it is hoped that it will eventually be possible to *alter* the response of the colony at will, and so for the first time actually *control* activities such as brood rearing, queen production, swarming and foraging.

Some progress has already been made. Seven components of the Nasonov pheromone of the worker honeybee have been identified. But only three of them are important in attracting swarming bees; furthermore, when these components are in equal proportions they are more attractive than when presented in the proportions in which they occur in the Nasonov gland. So we have a lure that is more attractive than the natural Nasonov pheromone. It should have a wide application in bee-keeping, and be particularly valuable in countries where absconding and migration are common occurrences.

It has also been demonstrated that it is possible to habituate honeybee colonies to their own alarm pheromones so that they become less aggressive. This could have important practical applications, especially in helping beekeepers to manipulate their more ferocious colonies.

Pheromones produced by the queen and brood stimulate foraging and, in particular, pollen collection. Other pheromones produced by foragers are used to attract recruits to beneficial crops. When these pheromones are identified, efforts will be made to use the synthetic pheromones to programme a colony's activities so that pollination is enhanced.

However, intensive and prolonged research will probably be necessary before our targets can be achieved, and more investment in equipment and research personnel is necessary to accelerate progress. But the likely rewards will be out of all proportion to the investment involved, and because the honeybee itself is cosmopolitan, the outcome will benefit honey and crop production and thus the living standards of man throughout the world.

150

Index

Numbers in italics refer to pages on which a relevant illustration also appears.

154